POUTINE

Poutine

A Deep-Fried Road Trip
of Discovery

Justin Giovannetti Lamothe

Douglas & McIntyre

DOUGLAS AND MCINTYRE (2013) LTD.
P.O. Box 219, Madeira Park, BC, VON 2HO
www.douglas-mcintyre.com

COVER IMAGE by Rosemarie Mosteller | Alamy
EDITED by Pam Robertson
COVER DESIGN by Jessica Sullivan | DSGN DEPT
TEXT DESIGN by Libris Simas Ferraz | Onça Publishing
PRINTED AND BOUND in Canada
PRINTED on 100% recycled paper

DOUGLAS AND MCINTYRE acknowledges the support of the Canada Council for the
Arts, the Government of Canada, and the Province of British Columbia through the
BC Arts Council.

LIBRARY AND ARCHIVES CANADA CATALOGUING IN PUBLICATION
Title: Poutine : a deep-fried road trip of discovery / Justin Giovannetti Lamothe.
Names: Lamothe, Justin Giovannetti, author.
Identifiers: Canadiana (print) 20240422244 | Canadiana (ebook) 20240422252 |
 ISBN 9781771624220 (softcover) | ISBN 9781771624237 (EPUB)
Subjects: LCSH: Poutine—Social aspects—Canada. | LCSH: Poutine—Social
 aspects—Québec (Province) | LCSH: Poutine—Canada—History. |
 LCSH: Poutine—Québec (Province)—History. | LCSH: Cooking, French-
 Canadian—History. | LCSH: Canada—Social life and customs. | LCSH: Québec
 (Province)—Social life and customs. | LCSH: National characteristics, Canadian.
Classification: LCC TX803.P8 L36 2024 | DDC 641.3/521—dc23

For Elio,
here's to making sure
your first poutine is memorable.

Table of Contents

New ground

THERE'S A DEEP PRIDE IN POUTINE. EVEN IN A CORNER OF THE world like Quebec where food is treated with an uncommonly elevated level of respect, poutine today isn't just any other dish. To a young restaurant owner ladling out glossy brown gravy from a steaming vat, poutine can be one of the strongest links to a family's culinary past. For the hungry patron who sits eyeing a plate piled high with fries, poutine can represent all that's good in their hometown. In the halls of academia, students and researchers can debate cheese curds with passion and reflect on how poutine has been transformed into a symbol, going so far as to work it into an argument about what defines the modern Quebec nation.

I didn't know any of that when I sat down across from my father on a frigid night in Montreal in 2013. There was a fresh layer of snow on the ground, and the cross on Mount Royal glowed in the distance through a frosty window. Families were out walking in a park across the street, and I could imagine the satisfying crunch of boots in the soft powder. The happy screams of children at play were muffled by the glass. The snow had started falling again.

"Tell me their names," my father said loudly, almost shouting. There was no menace or threat in his request—quite the opposite. He was so giddy that he was almost levitating out of his chair, his arms waving around as he spoke. His excitement and volume were growing with every syllable. I'd never seen him like this before. Over my lifetime I'd seen him happy and angry, and nearly every emotional state in between. But pure joy? Never.

"Poutine has always been one of my favourite things about Quebec," I had told him a few minutes earlier, trying to make conversation. I was scrambling. *Is that true?* I asked myself. *I have no idea. It's not totally untrue. Roll with it,* I answered with an internal shrug. I noticed he was paying close attention to my words.

"Just the smell of it reminds me of home and late nights with friends," I continued. *OK, that is true,* I told myself. Then to him: "You and I have also shared a few poutines over the years, and those are nice memories." He was nodding away.

"Yes, I like *une bonne poutine,*" my dad said with a smile, breaking the tension.

(One note of housekeeping: Nearly every interview in this book was conducted in French, including every interaction I had with my dad. In translating people's words, I've sought to keep their meanings and intentions more than any specific vocabulary. Where it makes sense, I've kept some of the flavour that each person brought to poutine's story. *On y va.*)

"But, you know," I told my dad. "I want to know more about the backstory of poutine. Beyond the basic facts I've already found online." That was also true. As a working journalist, I was always looking for story ideas, and this was one I was deeply interested in. My dad sat up straighter in his chair.

"What do you know about poutine?" he asked. Well, for one thing, it was the secret to a cheerful conversation with my father, as I was rapidly learning that night.

I had invited my dad to visit me because it was time for a talk I hadn't been looking forward to. The evening began with an awkward silence stretching out between the two of us. My parents had divorced years earlier, and my relationship with my dad had always been strained. I'd grown up in a bilingual household with an English-speaking mother in a deeply French city. I was a product of both worlds. Then I'd gone to school in English and worked in that language, while my dad remained proudly francophone. Further complicating the delicate cultural currents I was navigating on this night was the fact that I was in my early twenties and frankly had no idea what I was doing. Years of tension had culminated in this moment, and the dinner I'd prepared in my small kitchen was a last-ditch attempt at a reunion.

I'd accepted a great job in Toronto, and I'd just broken the news to him. "You're moving to Canada," he said after I finished speaking. The pasta on our plates was rapidly cooling. "Will Quebec see you again? Will I see you again?" he asked with real emotion slipping out.

For the past eight years, I'd lived in Montreal, which is a ninety-minute drive southwest of my hometown of Trois-Rivières, where my dad still lived. That was already tough enough for him psychologically, if not in reality, because he blanched at the idea of tangling in Montreal traffic and had never visited before tonight. In his mind, Toronto was a world away and a completely different country.

Putting aside the personal baggage from two lives that had rarely intersected in recent years, the conversation mirrored one that millions of Quebecers had already had in the past. For over a century, Quebecers have left their home province in large numbers for new homes in New England, Ontario and, more recently, Western Canada. That migration has left an indelible melancholy in some quarters of the provincial culture—something attested to in many well-thumbed copies of the classic novel *Thirty Acres*. Today, the 401 highway leading from Montreal to Toronto is still deeply rutted with the tracks of Quebecers who have left for greener pastures in politically fraught times.

The new job was a good career move for me but clearly struck my father as a choice to leave Quebec behind.

The thing about having two identities is that, in that moment, I was a francophone to him. Not only was I his son, but I was also a product of Quebec. Not irreplaceable on the provincial scale, but hard enough to replace as a son.

"Of course you'll see me again. It's only a few hours away," I told him unsteadily. He didn't look so sure. For years we'd kept up a casual dialogue with phone calls every few months that usually touched on how the Montreal Canadiens lineup was looking at that moment. The team was usually doing poorly, with little hope on the horizon. That level of superficial avoidance wouldn't do this time. As I looked for conversational inspiration on my plate, hoping to find a way to bury any suggestion of personal or provincial rejection, I began talking about poutine. There was nothing elegant about it—I just started babbling to answer my father's question about what I knew about poutine's past.

It was clear to me that a number of locals living in the Centre-du-Québec region south of Trois-Rivières had claimed to have invented the dish between the early 1950s and late 1960s. My dad perked up, moving to the edge of his plastic seat in my kitchen. "Centre-du-Québec! *Ah oui!* Tell me their names," he blurted out.

He began explaining why he wanted to know names. This is when I saw a side of my father emerge that I'd never seen before. The quiet man I'd struggled to connect with for the past half hour—and most of the two decades before it—had just left the room in a hurry. I realized then that I'd never had him tell me a story before. There was a tangible sense of pride as he became an impromptu storyteller. And what a story it was. I snapped a quick picture of him at that moment, his face in full delivery, arms waving around the room, but quickly put my phone away to focus on my dad. I was astonished and delighted by what I was seeing.

"I worked at a small *fromagerie* in Saint-Léonard-d'Aston in the sixties, and we made cheese curds. I started work early in the morning and drove to all the local farms to pick up milk jugs," he told me. "I spent a lot of time on all those roads in the Centre-du-Québec. We took that milk and made cheese curds. It's a very simple cheese. I made a lot of cheese curds in those days. That was in those years when poutine started. You can't have poutine without cheese curds."

My father has no claim to the history of poutine, but he may have had a very small support role alongside hundreds or thousands of others. He told me he might know who the inventors were. In the era when poutine was invented, in the region where it was invented, he worked at that *fromagerie*. If these small restaurants were ordering large amounts of fresh curds for their new poutines, he'd probably brought cheese to their kitchens at some point.

"But I don't remember eating poutine in those days. That came a bit later," he told me.

"Do you remember your first poutine?" I asked. I could see his mind racing off to another chapter in his past.

"Of course I remember my first."

Many Quebecers can remember their first poutines, and this would eventually become something akin to a rite of passage for a generation. Usually, it's a wispy story wrapped with youthful indiscretion, blossoming friendship and a helping of culinary bacchanalia. I would soon learn that my dad's first story happened earlier than most, and it brought us to a very different place than a Montreal apartment in the depths of winter. Instead, we had to go to a world where ears were deadened after a long afternoon of roaring stock-car engines, and the assembled stomachs of a young crowd were growling.

It's the early 1970s. We're at a small racetrack in central Quebec that isn't officially sanctioned yet, still just an oval of beaten dirt and clay set in lush farmland alongside the St. Lawrence River. Hours of hard turns and squealing tires that Sunday had left a cloud of thick dust hanging in the air, coating onlookers in a dirty film. That didn't stop local stalwarts like the three Tessier brothers from the village of Saint-Casimir from pushing their souped-up engines to the limit. Ronald was the favourite, while Normand and Robert were chasing their elder brother for the local stock-car crown. With a grin on his face and a steady pair of eyes, Ronald also had to hold off a bunch of other local drivers. There's no record of who won on that warm day—more noteworthy for our story is what happened after the race.

The spectators, including my dad, were mostly young locals who grew up on nearby farms or across the well-travelled waters of the *fleuve* in Trois-Rivières. (As a language, French can be quite specific, and *fleuve* is the word reserved for a river that empties into the ocean, of which the St. Lawrence is arguably the most well-known in Canada.) This race day was taking place during a time of great change. Quebec was in the throes of its Quiet Revolution, with people suddenly shaking off centuries of baggage and control by the Catholic clergy. On the grandstand, spectators sat between two real symbols of the conflict between the new and the old. To the north, the unfinished Laviolette Bridge, with its graceful arch carrying a new highway, soared over the St. Lawrence. What could be a better symbol of the modern era than a ribbon of asphalt that seemed to defy gravity? While to the south, the twin spires of the old Catholic church in Saint-Grégoire were no longer the most dominant structures in the region. The tall silver towers, built a century earlier, were receding in power and the popular imagination as church attendance fizzled.

The Quebecers of this area were living in a society on the move, with new ideas and money blazing into rural communities. The

American dream of plenty and getting good things faster, with fast food everywhere and good jobs to pay for it, was getting a makeover for Quebec—and locals were eager to sign up. Many of the young men and women at the track that day had grown up in demanding conditions, often on dairy farms little altered from those worked by their forefathers for generations. But suddenly that had changed, and they were now cheering on their favourite stock-car drivers, with more leisure time and money than their parents could have dreamt of only a decade earlier. Along with the new cars, snazzy fashion and two or three channels on their new televisions came a cornucopia of novel snacks.

When the race at the clay oval finished, the spectators filed into their cars and put their throaty American engines into gear. They were parched and hungry. As a crowd, they didn't have far to go. Only a few hundred metres down the road, turning indicators started blinking on. There was something new on the menu of the well-worn chip wagon alongside the road. Many customers would go for their trusted favourites, ordering a hot dog or hamburger with a side of fries. But some would try something a little more exotic that had appeared slowly over recent years.

My father, Laurent Lamothe, also stood outside the chip wagon in the gravel parking lot of the Fromagerie Descôteaux that day in the 1970s. Now, decades later, he would tell me about his first poutine, his mouth broadening an already wide smile between bites. "I'd heard some people mention it before the race. 'You need to go try a poutine there, at Descôteaux.' So that's what I did. Obviously it was good. The cheese was good. It was really fresh," he told me. "There's nothing quite like a first poutine, especially when you're hungry."

The word *poutine* wouldn't come to the area near the racetrack for many years, and debate continues today on its origin. In those days, on that particular menu, the dish was likely called a *mixte*. The

French word for mixed is a fairly self-explanatory, if blandly technical, description of poutine. But what did locals think as they picked up their orders for the first time? Was there shock at the mess of golden fries, the brown sauce glistening in the afternoon sun, the chunks of sweating cheese curds? Did it look like a mistake had been made with their order? There may have been a moment of hesitation before the aroma hit them. A poutine, freshly made, is both reassuringly warm and topped by a decadent scatter of fresh cheese.

Tearing into his poutine that day, spearing gravy-covered fries and curds from a styrofoam bowl with a plastic fork, my father discovered a new favourite. It's an experience many other Quebecers would share in the 1970s as the province's ubiquitous *casse-croûtes*, those small diners dotting the rural highways of that fast-modernizing society, added the dish to their menus. Most of the diners would have a local *fromagerie* nearby churning out cheese and butter. Sometimes in altered form, but often with little change, those small diners continue to be an indispensable part of Quebec's landscape to this day.

(A note on gravy: The French term for poutine gravy is *sauce*, and "poutine sauce" is a specific type of brown gravy sold at most Canadian grocers. This book uses the terms interchangeably, but know that, in Quebec English, it's nearly always a poutine sauce.)

Poutine is now seen as a nearly ever-present symbol of Quebec cuisine—possibly Canadian as well, depending on who you ask. Today, people around the world link poutine with Canada almost as strongly as they once did with the iconic red uniform of a Mountie. Poutine has even appeared on menus, alongside a small maple leaf, in the Australian outback and at a White House state dinner.

Back in my apartment, my dad took a moment to sip his water. Our plates hadn't been touched in minutes, growing cold as we ignored them. Instead, he'd been speaking as rapidly as the words came to him.

I was left largely as a spectator, one who was very happy with the price of admission, nodding and taking mental notes. While he took his sip, I snuck in a question.

"Poutine feels comfortably permanent now. But all things start somewhere. I really want to know exactly where that new food you'd just tried came from," I said.

"I think it came from Drummondville or somewhere near there. Some people say Victoriaville," my dad told me. Both are small cities in central Quebec.

"But why would it have come from either of those places?" I asked.

"I think it's because you need local ingredients. It's an agricultural area, and there are lots of farmers around there," he said, now deeply in thinking mode. It was a good start, but we'd need more. A lot more. Someone invented poutine, and we'd have to find them.

A plan began forming in the back of my mind. We'd need to go on a road trip, to first map and then follow the trail poutine left across Quebec. Trying to definitively nail down the inventor of poutine had been something of a sport among Quebec journalists for decades, but I had an inside man.

"OK. We need to go on a drive and find out. You're the secret weapon here," I told him.

He smiled, a warm and deep smile that went right up to the corners of his eyes. "I'd really like that," he said.

"I'll be coming back to Quebec, and I'm going to share this journey with you. You've got a good insurance policy there that I'll be back," I told my dad, trying to match his smile with my own excitement.

"I might know a good guy to talk to. He's a Descôteaux. I think he was there near the beginning," he said seriously. My dad was all in.

This poutine-centred caper would be a departure from the norm for us. We hadn't really been on a long drive alone before—some family trips when I was a kid, but that was years before my parents separated. Smiles stayed on our faces as we started talking about where we'd need to go.

The next morning, I helped push his car out of a snowbank and he headed back to Trois-Rivières. But we parted on a cheerful note. I'd made a promise: while I might be headed away to Ontario soon, I'd be coming back.

It would take years before we finally got the timing right. Our phone calls started changing—the chats about hockey were bolstered by any poutine tidbits either of us had picked up here and there. I moved six times in a decade for work, but our newly shared journey into poutine's history became something constant we could return to. While we never set up a picture board in a garage with our ideas joined by red yarn, the strands became increasingly taut in our minds.

While we thought we'd find the people who created poutine, we found a lot more. This became a way to bridge a cultural divide and help repair a relationship that had grown thin through misunderstanding and neglect. We also found out a lot more than we bargained for about poutine.

This is the story of poutine's life, from its unassuming birth decades ago, through its vigorous adolescence, into its mature years as a national symbol. For the moment, all we knew was that poutine is a delightful food, a well-tested hangover cure and an internationally recognized symbol of Canada.

It was early summer in 2017 when I first set out from Toronto and left my now-wife behind for the start of this poutine adventure. The story would evolve slowly over the years that followed, delayed by work and the pandemic, but it remained a growing link between the two of us.

For that first drive, my dad and I had a very rough plan of where we needed to go to find poutine's birthplace and an idea of where to locate some of the people who might have made it happen. My dad hadn't been to some of the places we wanted to visit in over a half century, but he was sure he'd find them.

The day we planned to head out, I found him in the backyard of the home where I'd grown up, covered in grime and on his back welding together the busted frame of a friend's pickup truck. Occasional welding kept him busy in retirement, and he'd done odd jobs for everyone from Montreal Canadiens players to members of the local chapter of the Hells Angels motorcycle gang—who were always very polite and left a hefty tip.

"Hello boy! Is that today?" he said as he dusted himself off and came over to greet me. We decided on a one-day delay.

The next morning, we pulled out of his driveway in his beaten-up Ford sedan. There was welding equipment covering the back seat that looked like it hadn't been moved in ages, as well as a measuring tape in each cupholder that needed to be plucked out to make room for coffee. To my surprise, the sounds of Adele suddenly came out of his CD player.

"Really?" I asked in surprise. He had always been more of a classic Quebec rock kind of guy.

He shrugged. "It's good," he said in English, unapologetically, as "Rolling in the Deep" started up in the background. *Let it play*, I thought.

We rolled south over the busy Laviolette Bridge, toward the yellowing fields and rural roads of the south shore that my dad had called home long before I came into his life. The green paint was peeling off the bridge, and the road was covered in potholes that rattled the car. "This is a perfect day for this drive," he said, looking out over the flatlands in the distance. I could see in his eyes that we were also moving back in time.

Somewhere ahead of us was where one of Canada's best-known dishes had emerged. We had to find it. "Where are we going first?" I asked. He pointed ahead. We took the first exit off the highway.

CHAPTER ONE

"It's a taste of home"

MY DAD IS BEHIND THE WHEEL AS WE PULL INTO THE PARKING lot outside the Roy Jucep in the small city of Drummondville, Quebec. The restaurant is as close to a mecca for poutine as you can find, with many in the province convinced it is the birthplace of the iconic dish. It feels like a good place to start.

My father stares at the parking lot, seemingly surprised that this place has been around since the 1960s. He's been to Drummondville hundreds of times since he was a teenager. "I've never seen this place before," he says, looking around curiously at the restaurant and its big orange slice. "Are you sure this is an old place?"

We're here because even a rudimentary Google search reveals that the Roy Jucep has a long history with poutine, and my dad was convinced before we hit the road that Drummondville was likely where the whole thing started.

"Wait a minute," he says after more contemplation. "Yes, I have! This used to be a drive-in." His eyes dart around as the memory slots into place. "We'd come here with my brother and some girls in my big car, a full car, after going to the cinema." A smile slides onto his face. "They'd have girls bring over your food on a tray and clip it to the side here," he says, motioning at the driver's side window. "I was a young man and they were pretty girls. They had short skirts, I remember that."

I nod. I'd come across some of that in my research. Decades ago, carhops rushed back and forth between patrons waiting in their vehicles. Whatever the weather, they scurried out with warm orders and clipped metal trays to the sides of cars. That service is now long gone, but we're clearly in the right place.

Like many restaurants that have been around for decades, the Roy Jucep is an institution with some idiosyncrasies. The decor is both retro and modern, with a large orange slice on the roof beckoning motorists on one of Drummondville's busiest streets. It's a clear throwback to an earlier age when the restaurant first made its name.

This is the first stop on our road trip that has food, and we are ready to eat. After stepping out of the car and stretching our legs, the first hint of poutine is in the air before we even get inside the restaurant. "You saw all those farms just outside of Drummondville. This is still a good area for cheese—it isn't what it once was, but it's going to be fresh cheese curds in there. Now I'm hungry," my dad says, moving toward the door. We'd just driven through the heart of Quebec dairy country, the green, brown and yellow fields broken up by tidy farmhouses and the occasional small town. Every few minutes, another set of spires on a Catholic church would pop into view. Desjardins credit unions also dotted the landscape. Both institutions are present in nearly every village, looking only slightly different from the pair a few kilometres down the road.

We'd started out earlier that morning in Trois-Rivières. Our first stop was supposed to be the racetrack where my dad had eaten his first poutine, but something else had caught our eye. There was a tourism information centre right off the highway where we happened to take the first exit at the town of Bécancour. A massive Acadian flag fluttered above the small building.

"That place might have some helpful information," I told my dad.

He shrugged and pulled into the parking lot. "I've never been here," he said.

While I'm not a food writer by trade—despite the increasingly ample evidence to the contrary—one of my first stories while working in Ontario was about food. In 2013, I wrote about another classic Canadian comfort food: the butter tart. I'd gotten a tip that two Ontario municipal governments were headed toward a courtroom showdown over who could claim the bragging rights to butter tart tourism. What I discovered was a battle between a rich community east of Toronto, where many of the city's wealthy own weekend cottages, and a hardscrabble township home to a large working-class population and lots of local pride. One operated a website promoting a Butter Tart Trail, the other had pamphlets offering a Butter Tart Tour—and the civic disagreement between the municipalities was getting out of hand. Lawyers were trading threats and a court date was looming. I spent a day driving between the two communities, speaking with the owners of local restaurants and getting a personal introduction to butter tarts when I was invited to help cook up a batch. I wrote a few hundred words and, after my story appeared on the front page of *The Globe and Mail*, the two municipalities promptly shook the egg off their collective faces and decided they could coexist. Each could continue to hawk butter tarts to passing tourists.

That story comes back to me now as we walk into the tourism centre. Could someone in Quebec have dreamt up a Poutine Trail? There isn't one, I quickly discover. The walls are covered in flyers about vineyards and cycling, as well as ads for a wide selection of bed and breakfasts. Agrotourism and tours of autumn foliage are well represented. But for all the prospect of leaf peeping, there's no mention of poutine.

I ding a bell inside the tourism centre. "Has anyone ever come inquiring about poutine's history and where they should go to find where it came from?" I ask the man who comes up to the counter.

He is fastidiously dressed and likely in his late sixties. "Never! You're the first. There always needs to be a first," he says with a big smile and commendable cheer for the morning hour.

My dad walks up and introduces himself: "I'm Laurent Lamothe, this is my son, and he's going to write about the history of poutine." I hear an echo of that excitement from when we'd first talked about tracing the dish's roots. He is on his own poutine trail, and enjoying it.

The man's interest is immediately piqued and he introduces himself as Clement Prince. He explains that he is from Princeville, a hamlet outside the nearby town of Victoriaville.

"You know, Princeville is the home of poutine," he says. Both my father and I let out an "*ah ouain*" of surprise at the same time. "Poutine started in the late 1950s. There was a lot of cheese curds and a lot of fries around this area. A trucker stopping at a local diner ordered it up and poured some gravy on it. I always heard, growing up, that that happened in Princeville," he says.

As I'd learn over the course of the day, this type of serendipitous exposition is not at all unusual in the Centre-du-Québec region. It was impressive that, unprompted, Prince had provided what turned out to be a fairly accurate history of poutine. I take out a notepad and begin writing, and he adds more details as he keeps speaking. While some of the information may be biased toward his hometown, he spins a good yarn.

That's when I notice my dad is shifting his weight from foot to foot. He finally breaks in: "What about Drummondville? I'd always heard it was Drummondville. I was here in those years, and I don't remember a big restaurant scene in Princeville." My dad's tone is one of suspicion.

"Ah, don't listen to the other claims. Every small roadside *casse-croûte* around here claims they were first," says Prince, undaunted and still cheerful. With a dismissive wave, he tells us Princeville is the real deal.

"Do you know where we might be able to get a poutine in Princeville, where it was first served?" I ask. I notice my father giving me side-eye for the first time in my life. Before that moment, I didn't think he even knew what side-eye was.

Prince is happy to oblige and helpfully provides us with the names of diners near the one he claims invented the dish—the original had closed decades earlier, he says. He wishes us luck, and we make our goodbyes and head out the door.

Safely outside, my father is having none of it. "There's not *une criss de chance* that poutine was invented in Princeville."

Francophone pop plays on the radio as we start off again. While we'd originally taken this exit for the racetrack, that would have to wait. "I skipped breakfast. I'm getting a little hungry," my dad says. But we shouldn't head for Princeville yet, we decide. While the small town may have played a role in poutine's history—that's my charitable interpretation, my dad's is still a flat no—it's best to start where the trail is still warm. Poutine, my father is convinced, came from Drummondville, which is just forty-five minutes away.

My dad forgets the little plastic tab and pulls the entire top off his cup of coffee from Tim Hortons, the first of many, and begins narrating the world around this dusty rural highway as we head south. Large, modern farms and small houses zoom past, but his words and images go back decades, to the farmers and families of his youth. "That's Mr. Beauchemin," he tells me, pointing toward a farmhouse. "He's got cows." This goes on consistently as we drive, a verbal map overlaid on the world outside of what is and what had been.

Decades earlier, when Quebec was a younger province, my father was at the wheel of a rusty old GMC truck that rattled down these roads to local farms where he picked up cans of milk. He shifts back to the present, describing the scene. "But Mr. Gauthier across the street over there has hundreds more cows," he carries on. The car heads toward the centreline of the road as his attention is solidly away from the driving. I give him a poke. We speed past a series of small homes, with wide porches and tin roofs. I imagine myself back in the late 1950s, puttering along and listening to Quebec crooner Félix Leclerc crackling on the radio, clutching a paper bag full of fresh cheese curds.

You might not notice it when you first walk into the Roy Jucep, with its gaudy decor and brightly polished steel drawing your eye to the restaurant's bustling counter. A server might move past with a tray of poutine that demands your attention. But the one place your eye won't be drawn is a small piece of paper in a simple black frame hanging by the door. As our unexpected debate at the tourism centre showed, poutine is serious business in Quebec. The dish sometimes approaches the status of the Montreal Canadiens as an unofficial religion, and the frame contains a powerful document. It's a federal certificate stating that the Roy Jucep holds the trademark as "poutine's inventor." While many in Quebec have spent decades fighting perceived—and real—overreach from bureaucrats in Ottawa, this small stamp of approval from the federal government has few opponents. Even Quebec's representatives in the National Assembly, usually happy to pick a fight with Ottawa, have been content to leave the story of poutine's birth to federal authorities.

Moments after we walk into *le Jucep*, as locals often call it, a spirited argument erupts at a nearby booth about whether poutine really came from the restaurant. Names of nearby towns start coming up. There's some indignation and heated words. "It was Warwick… It was Victoriaville." Eyebrows dance as tempers flare. A waitress points to the certificate and clears her throat with the self-assured grunt of a heavyweight boxer. Silence falls as it's read, and a few impressed whistles tumble out. "This happens almost every day," she tells me later. "People love to argue about it, but the certificate ends that." It's a powerful piece of paper. And yes, it has been stolen repeatedly over the years.

The Roy Jucep's story began in the late 1950s, when a young Jean-Paul Roy returned to his native Drummondville from Montreal. Only twenty-three, Roy had spent the previous six years as a cook in the basement of Montreal's stately Mount Royal Hotel. It was one of the largest hotels in the British Empire at the time, with over one thousand guest rooms and several grand chandeliers dominating the common spaces. Decades later, the hotel would be gutted and become the upscale Les Cours Mont-Royal shopping centre.

Armed with experience turning out food for a demanding audience quickly, Roy opened a small *casse-croûte* in downtown Drummondville called Le Roy de la Patate. He'd learned to make a gravy in Montreal that was the cornerstone of his new venture. The eponymously named fry shack was a play on words, with the name Roy having the same pronunciation in French as the word *roi*, meaning king. So the roadside fry joint was the "King of the Potato." Roy and his wife, Fernande, started offering gravy to customers along with the fries. Bags of fresh cheese curds also appeared for sale on the counter where patrons placed their orders. Business was booming and, in 1964, Roy bought an ice cream bar called the Orange Jucep. The orange was quickly dropped from the name, if not from the roof of the building, and the Roy Jucep was born.

We haven't made it far past the door into the Roy Jucep, and my father and I wave to a server at the same time. There's excitement in the air. She points at a nearby booth and we slip into place. Every wall in the joint is dripping with poutine history. It feels like the right place to have your first poutine while searching for the dish's story. It's late morning and the lunch rush hasn't come in yet, but the restaurant is already filling up. In what's quickly becoming his standard operating procedure, my dad makes introductions and explains we aren't two usual diners. "Alright," the waitress says with a shrug. "We've had so many people come here over the years for a story. But you're lucky, Yolande is in today."

While most people connected to the early days of poutine have moved along or passed away, Yolande Morissette is still around. Now in her early seventies, Morissette first put on the diner's uniform in 1968 when she was fourteen years old. She's seen generations of Drummondville locals grow up as they frequented the Roy Jucep. She slips into an empty chair beside us.

"We sold a lot of poutine. From the beginning. A lot. I always used to ask myself why people would order a big poutine and a Diet Pepsi," she tells me with a chuckle. Not only has she worked here for decades, but she's a hardened waitress who calls them like she sees them. She relaxes into her story—this is going to be a break from an otherwise busy shift. "The first chef to throw it together, we called him Ti-Pout. He started it. I don't remember his name," Morissette says. *Ti-Pout* is Québécois slang for short guy. "He started just putting the cheese curds, fries and sauce together. Some of the patrons told him to give it a name. One of the other cooks said, 'Why don't you call it poutine?' I forget the second cook's name too. One day I really need to think about it," she adds. "I never really knew Ti-Pout. We have a photo of him somewhere. He certainly wasn't a big man."

Fernande Michaud-Roy, Roy's wife and the restaurant's cofounder, identified Ti-Pout as a local named Gilles Dubé in an interview with Drummondville's newspaper in 2021. The trail to find him has gone cold.

According to the mythology of poutine's invention, now printed on the back of the Roy Jucep's menu, this is roughly how the approved story goes. The exact day when the first modern poutine was made is unknown, but it arose from public demand. In the 1960s, the Roy Jucep had quickly become a favourite spot at night for revellers looking to douse an evening of drinking with a dollop of grease. It's likely the dish was created when somewhat pickled clients coming out of nearby bars would order fries, ask for Roy's delicious gravy to be ladled overtop and then, finally, ask the chef to throw some cheese curds on as well. Fries, cheese and sauce combined would be easier to carry in unsteady hands. This likely first happened around 1964, soon after the Roy Jucep opened. What isn't made clear on the plastic-covered menu is that once poutine was first ordered in Drummondville, it became an instant hit.

For both waitresses and clients, "poutine" became an easier shorthand than what they'd been using since the first gooey mess came out, which was some version of: "Could I have an order of fries, cheese and sauce together?" The likely inspiration, Morissette tells us, was either the English word *pudding* ("It sounds a bit like it," she says) or a definition of poutine from the day that meant a mess. With chefs always teasing each other in the kitchen, as Morissette remembers, what may have once been a joke about "Ti-Pout's pudding" rapidly became poutine.

The history and meaning of the name itself remain contentious. In the end, Morissette says, there was an informal meeting in 1964, and the restaurant's staff decided to pull down the menu and make the new shorthand official. They put the menu back up with the word *poutine* on it. The word and its usage quickly spread throughout

Drummondville. That meeting, and the fact that poutine now clearly denoted the mix of the three ingredients we know today, became the basis of the federal trademark hanging on the Roy Jucep's wall.

Morissette has witnessed poutine's journey from a late-night favourite to a globally recognized symbol of Canada. But while she's proud of the restaurant, and will happily—and fiercely—defend Roy's contribution to cuisine, Morissette shrugs at the scope of what might have been invented here. Instead, she prefers to remember the man fondly.

"I was only fourteen when I started. I worked on Friday, Saturday and Sunday. But only during the mornings on Sunday. Mr. Roy didn't want me at work in the evening. He wanted me to be studying at home," Morissette remembers. "Mr. Roy didn't want me to walk around the block when I finished at 4 a.m., so he made a hole in the fence behind the restaurant that let me pop over right into my parents' backyard. He was my father's best friend and wanted to look out for me."

Morissette didn't always work at the Roy Jucep. After school, she left to start a daycare, took a detour to work in a light bulb plant, owned a bar and then left that job pretty quickly. When Roy asked her to come back a few decades ago, she was happy to oblige. She hasn't left since.

My father is nodding along—and salivating, partly because we haven't eaten yet and poutines keep coming out of the kitchen. "I think I remember coming here in those early days," he tells her. "Did you guys used to have the carhops with the roller skates?"

She shakes her head at the question. "Carhops, yes. But no, you wouldn't want to see me in roller skates." Unlike his more combative exchange earlier in the morning with Prince, he's listening to Morissette intently.

I ask her about other claims, like whether Princeville came first. "People in Warwick are pretty adamant, but it was Mr. Roy," she says firmly.

She exhales deeply and looks around the restaurant. Surrounded by pictures of what once was and talking about the past, Morissette seems to be feeling a lot of nostalgia. Things have changed and not always for the better, in her mind. "When Mr. Roy ran the place, we made a lot here. We made our own desserts, lots of sugar pies and our own strawberry jam. We even made the dough for Pogos. We used to make the fish and chips here as well," she says. "We don't make that anymore, they just buy it. Everything has changed so much." This isn't the world that created poutine.

To get a better sense of the forces at work in the 1960s, I call Jean-Philippe Warren after my trip to Drummondville. A professor at Montreal's Concordia University, he's the research chair for the study of Quebec. Warren is one of the country's experts on the decades around the province's Quiet Revolution. This was a period of intense social, economic and political change after 1960 that rapidly transformed Quebec, with a modern, secular and French-speaking state established over just a few years. Before the Quiet Revolution, many of Quebec's central institutions were still controlled by the Catholic Church.

Warren tells me there was a fascination in the province at the time with everything American. French Canadians wanted what they saw reflected in the strutting colossus to the south, including the fast cars, the glamour of Hollywood movies, the new industries and the promise of prosperity. For Quebecers, this love affair was often expressed through food.

"In Quebec, you started seeing many fast-food venues all over the province. The hot dog, the hamburger and french fries became a very big thing for the working class. This was seen as a way for them to claim that American dream. It seems weird that by eating a hot dog you would be part of that ethos, but it was seen as that at the time," Warren tells me.

Despite the changes rocking Quebec society, there was no move to copy the United States wholesale. Instead, Quebecers wanted a world that was faster and more modern but still distinctly French Canadian. Those two ideals, along with the tension that sometimes causes friction between them, continue in Quebec to this day.

"It was a time of great national pride, and there was a wave of new French-Canadian nationalism. The old French-Canadian nationalism had been turned to the past and people's ancestors. It was very rural. It celebrated life with priests in the little villages," says Warren. "The 1940s, '50s and '60s saw the rise of a new form of nationalism that wanted to build a modern Quebec. But it was always going to be in French, always French Canadian and structured within the French-Canadian community. It was very close-knit but modern. It was basically about things staying exactly like they've always been, except with a Buick in your driveway, a bungalow for a home and a box of Kellogg's in the kitchen."

The seeming paradox of seeking to change everything, while basically ensuring everything stays the same, could be seen at the Roy Jucep's lunch counter in the 1960s. The restaurant would feel comfortable, with a warm Québécois greeting on the way in, while everything about it would be absolutely new. Poutine itself was a way to bridge those two worlds, combining the speedy efficiency of the American dream in its preparation, all mixed in a dish based on familiar local ingredients.

Jean-Paul Roy and Fernande Michaud-Roy rode that wave of change. They managed the Roy Jucep for over two decades after they opened it, splitting responsibilities for the restaurant. He continued to be the skilled saucier that pulled in patrons and was the public face of the joint, while she helped ensure everything was orderly and kept the books in shape. After years of countless long days and the lifting of bags of potatoes, gravy and cheese, the two retired. What they left was a Jucep that has become a pillar of the local community—it's the kind of restaurant where local businesses still proudly advertise on the placemats. Locals carry the name of the restaurant with pride wherever they go.

After the Roys sold, local Yves Larocque bought the restaurant. However, he kept the keys to poutine's kingdom for only three years. His ownership is now largely forgotten, omitted from most histories of the restaurant. Another local, Daniel Leblanc, then owned it for most of the next quarter century. He expanded the Roy Jucep and modernized it as times changed. The two founders are no longer part of the Jucep today. Jean-Paul died nearly two decades ago, while Fernande is still in Drummondville but has grown tired of giving interviews about the history of poutine. She says she'd rather be swinging a golf club at the local course.

The flow of customers is picking up at the Roy Jucep, and there's some yelling in the nearby kitchen. Morissette excuses herself and sets off to help. I catch my dad looking over at where she's heading, and his eyes track the poutines as they come out. "The cheese looks good here. But it's not as good as the cheese we used to make at the *fromagerie*," he tells me.

Visiting that *fromagerie* was on our itinerary, but first we wanted to chat with more people in Drummondville. One of those locals was Renée Brousseau. A former manager at the Roy Jucep, she's lived in the city since she was thirteen.

She came to the restaurant to meet us after I messaged her. After a quick wave to the waitress by the front door, she sits down in the recently vacated seat. Brousseau is middle-aged, with dark brown hair and wearing a simple black T-shirt. She gives off an air of no-nonsense and confidence. Her history here goes back far, she tells us. Her first poutine was at the Jucep. "Most people who grew up around here have a similar childhood memory. It's a fact of life growing up in Drummondville. Everyone has come here," she says.

The Jucep's success isn't for a lack of competitors. It sits in the middle of a town with an incredibly varied selection of poutine options. In this oasis of curds, many swear by the hearty servings from another local institution, the Fromagerie Lemaire. Not only does that *fromagerie* make its own cheese curds and specialize in turning out poutine, but it also has locations on the two main highways. You really can't get into Drummondville without driving past one of the Lemaire locations. While the architecture isn't as unmistakable as the Jucep's large orange slice, Lemaire's garish paint is instantly recognizable.

Living in Drummondville, locals can forget that bad poutine exists. Brousseau says she has horror stories from the rest of Canada. "I remember having a poutine a few years ago in Toronto and it came with mozzarella on it. *Câliboire*," Brousseau says with a laugh. "That's not very good."

My dad jumps in: "I ate a poutine in Alberta with cheese that had been frozen. It wasn't very good. In other places, it feels like they can't get the fries or gravy right. It's nice to have all these options here, isn't it?"

Like many locals, it takes little prompting for Brousseau to launch into the debate about where poutine originally emerged. She likens it to the hockey rivalry that once existed between the NHL teams in Montreal and Quebec City. "It's friendly," she says, "but people are fervent in their beliefs." I mention the conversation we had with Clement Prince at the tourism information booth. She nods.

"That rivalry is one of the reasons there's no officially endorsed poutine tourism in Quebec," she says. "If you named four or five restaurants at the tourism kiosk that people should try, that would be favouring them. It's a touchy subject."

As Brousseau sees it, everyone keeps the peace by naming no one. When I mention that most online searches about poutine's past lead to restaurants in Montreal, she shudders. "It's not a Montreal dish." There's a blizzard's worth of chill in her voice.

Unbeknownst to Brousseau, I discovered later that Drummondville actually has tried to capitalize on its poutine roots in the recent past. In 2015, the city launched a tourism campaign featuring local radio host Frédéric Bastien Forrest offering poutine to people in New York City, Panama City and Tokyo. Why those three places? Who knows. Watching the material later, I'm struck that the entire thing has a bit of a frantic feeling to it. It's less about the "birthplace" of poutine—that's just a hook to get people in. Instead, the final product is about cracking jokes about what Drummondville offers. Equal parts endearing and cringe-inducing, the campaign has largely been relegated to history and the Drummondville municipal archives.

After we finish chatting, Brousseau gets up and heads out—carrying an order of poutine, of course. Morissette comes back over, and I really want to know more about those early years when she was a waitress. My dad and I are too engulfed in the conversation to remember we haven't eaten yet.

Morissette is not sure what else to add. The hardest days at the restaurant were when customers would come over after the stock-car races in the late 1960s. "It was hell," she says. "Customers would line up outside right out to the street. They'd park big cars and start honking for us to come out and serve them at the wheel. It wouldn't stop until 4 a.m. At least, that's when I went home." The local police would be expecting the call and would come ready for crowd control. Outside, as many officers as could be spared would be busy keeping the street cleared of backed-up traffic and drunken patrons stumbling in front of cars. Over fifty years later, you can still feel the mayhem as she describes what the carnival-like atmosphere was like on a weekly basis.

Morissette adds that the scene inside the restaurant was not much better. Despite a full staff, with a kitchen jammed with cooks working shoulder to shoulder and a full crew of servers running a non-stop flow of Pepsi and milkshakes out the door, everyone would come away exhausted and covered in sweat. But the chaos was profitable. Poutine put the Roy Jucep on the map, helped generations of staff put their kids through university and paid for a series of major expansions that took a rudimentary fry shack on the side of the road and turned it into a beloved icon.

The days of the late-night rush are over. Reflecting modern social trends, the restaurant now closes just after midnight on weekends, and earlier during the week. However, there's still a small taste of what once was, with patrons from nearby bars squeezing in before last call. Poutine's status as the king of late-night snacks is undisputed, but it would be wrong to think of it as only that. As is clearly evidenced around us, a steady drumbeat of orders keeps things hopping. "People order poutine after a night shift, early in the morning, they order it at noon, they order it at night. People are poutine eaters," says Morissette, who is well placed to come to that conclusion after four decades at the restaurant.

Like many in Drummondville, she won't eat poutine anywhere else. Following my father and Brousseau before her, she brings up unprompted that she still cringes at the idea of eating a poutine in English Canada. "I'm difficult when it comes to the cheese. It has to be right. I won't have it anywhere else but in Quebec. It needs to be fresh, it needs to go squish. You just need that," she says with conviction.

While she'll finally put down the apron and retire one day, Morissette isn't worried about the place she's given so much of her life to. "The Roy Jucep's future is set in stone," she says. "It's a symbol for me. I've seen it in every way. I saw it when I was small and the restaurant was very small. It's now the one unmistakable part of Drummondville. Everyone knows the Jucep. They know the big orange. There are plenty of restaurants in this city. Many of them have poutine, but we invented poutine." She gets up and starts walking around the restaurant, telling us to follow. She stops, takes down pictures that interest her from the walls and talks about how things have changed since this or that image was snapped.

We get to the certificate by the front door and the tension of who came first. I tell her about the debate when we walked in and how it ended swiftly. She smiles. The main argument rests on two men, she explains—Drummondville's Jean-Paul Roy and Warwick's Fernand Lachance. "I always point to the certificate. People are always bickering about whether it's Drummondville or Warwick. In Warwick, it was Mr. Lachance. Here in Drummondville, it was Mr. Roy. They are both dead. The restaurant in Warwick doesn't exist anymore, and we are still here and have the certificate." She stops for a moment and delivers a shrug that suggests there's no room for argument. "We are still here. So people pose with it. They tell me they want to take it home and show it to friends," she continues. The deeper argument is irrelevant to her. There's no debate in Morissette's mind: "Of course we invented poutine. Of course. That's final."

With that, we shake her hand and thank her for what has turned into an impromptu tour. My father and I return to the booth near the front door of the Roy Jucep where we'd been a few minutes earlier. There's an orange glow from the restaurant's colour of choice. The most recent renovations, only a few years earlier, added trendy accents to the vintage 1950s interior. The chairs are clean orange leather, while globe lights with the restaurant's name etched into the frosted glass hang from above.

But we're not here for the interior design, regardless of how well they've pulled it off. There's something missing from this pew in the cathedral of poutine: the dish itself. We've been good and patient, but the rumbling of our stomachs is now unmistakable. "I think it's time we order," I tell my dad. His nod is emphatic.

Two menus are quickly slipped onto our table, and the poutine page isn't hard to find. While Roy might have first put a poutine on the menu, the choices at the restaurant have expanded significantly in the past decades. There are now twenty-six options, ranging from the authentic for $9.95, to a pizza poutine topped with pepperoni, green peppers, mushrooms, tomato sauce and mozzarella cheese. While I consider the Oktoberfest for a split second—a German sausage is added to the mix—I'm really here for the authentic. They've been making it for fifty years. Two orders go out, to be accompanied by two glasses of Pepsi.

The drinks and poutines arrive a few minutes later. The dish looks absolutely mouthwatering, and neither of us hesitates to grab our forks and dig in. The aroma is instant and inviting. The fries are done just right, browned and a little crispy but still thick enough to hold the dish together. The sauce is oddly sweet for a poutine but pleasantly highlights the cheese. The curds are truly magnificent. They are the size of banana chunks and dripping fresh. As I bite into them, they are so fresh that they squeak with absolute abandon. It's so loud it reminds me of a bicycle stopping in the rain. And there's a lot of squeaking because the fry-to-cheese ratio is about one-to-one. The three ingredients mix with every bite, each balancing the other and delivering a flavourful punch. With each bite, I focus on a different note, like the little bit of tanginess in the sauce or the crunch of the fries. This might be one of the best poutines I've ever had, and it leaves me beyond satisfied, floating on an ocean of bliss. My dad and I just look at each other and nod—no words are necessary to describe how superb it is.

Making poutine at this level of quality is a surprisingly complicated process. Once you throw in the significant quantities coming out of the kitchen every day, the Roy Jucep isn't just a restaurant: it's a poutine assembly line. I peer into the kitchen and see a blur of activity. There's a buzz as plates are passed around and scalding hot machines make loud noises, demanding attention. Suzanne Lussier is spinning around grabbing ingredients to mix together a poutine. The sixty-one-year-old could make a poutine blindfolded. "It's all weighed in advance. The cheese here is eighty-six grams," she says, ripping open a bag from a nearby *fromagerie* and dumping it onto a plate of fries. Then she grabs a ladle of gravy and pours it on. "I've worked here for fifteen years," she says. A machine behind her begins buzzing again—she works some knobs and silences it. "We make a lot of poutine every day. I don't eat very much of it. Maybe from time to time I'll eat one, but not me, not really." Another machine's alarm goes off—it sounds like a heart monitor on a patient who isn't doing too well. "I've been making poutine since I was sixteen. I used to own my own restaurant, so I know this pretty well," she says, pushing the finished plate toward a waitress and moving on to another poutine. The kitchen's buzz won't be stopping for hours. "And the Jucep makes the best poutine," she adds, a bead of sweat on her forehead.

Before we leave, we spot some diners having a good laugh together. My dad heads over to chat with them. Violette Beaudoin quickly tells us she knows how lucky she is to have the Jucep as a reliable option for lunch. She and two friends have settled into a corner booth. Beaudoin, Annie Brouillard and Monique Doiron have walked over from their nearby work. The three of them are in matching uniforms, with white dress shirts and black vests. Beaudoin is the oldest of the three, in her sixties, with her glasses resting on her head. Sitting in front of each of them is a steaming bowl of poutine. What else could you want in life?

"It's a taste of home. They don't make it the same anywhere else," Beaudoin says with a happy sigh. When she gets back to her hometown from a vacation, she heads to the Roy Jucep to get a poutine to ground herself. If she can't make it over, she'll order one to her home. Either way, she's getting poutine. "We all know the number by heart," she adds with a laugh. The restaurant's delivery drivers are kept busy around the clock in this industrious city. Like many in Drummondville, she's proud of poutine's local heritage.

The three women sip on bottles of Diet Pepsi as they eat. For complicated reasons of history and catchy advertising, Quebecers are some of the few people in the world who reliably prefer Pepsi over Coca-Cola.

The three of them enjoy different things about poutine. They giggle and cut each other off as they talk about the dishes in front of them. The youngest of the three, Brouillard, loves the cheese. "The cheese that goes squeak-squeak, that's the best," she exclaims, pointing to the curds on her dish. She's ordered her poutine with a helping of extra cheese curds, which means the little white blobs absolutely crowd the top of her bowl. Flowing around the three, a late lunch rush is starting to slow down. While the restaurant has other items on its menu, the word *poutine* is almost as thick in the air as the sauce being ladled onto the servings.

"The Roy Jucep makes the best poutine in Quebec, *point final*," says Doiron. "If you want to argue with that, I hope you did your homework," she adds.

I put my hands up in surrender. "What makes it the best?" I ask.

"The poutine here, really the whole restaurant, reminds me of visits to the Jucep when I was a young girl, decades ago."

Unlike the other two, she ordered one of the better-known variants of poutine. It's called a *galvaude*, and many of Quebec's poutine restaurants have a version of it on the menu. Along with the usual fries and gravy, a *galvaude* comes with green peas and chunks of shredded chicken. Some restaurants keep the cheese curds, while others dispense with them entirely.

The Roy Jucep's *galvaude* doesn't have curds, but it does add a large helping of creamy coleslaw on top. To Doiron, it's perfection.

CHAPTER TWO

Of cows and curds

A S MY FATHER AND I LEAVE THE ROY JUCEP AND HOP BACK INTO his car, I start thinking about an overseas adventure in poutine-making from a few years back. In the summer of 2015, I travelled to East Africa on vacation. While trekking through the savannah, a question occurred to me: how hard could it be for three Canadians to make a poutine in Africa? My two friends from Montreal and I set out to answer that question.

I'd arrived days earlier in Tanzania with a Montreal care package: six St-Viateur bagels and a packet of dried poutine sauce from the St-Hubert rotisserie restaurant. The bagels went first, then came time for the poutine. The gravy would be easy: just add water and it tastes like you're in Quebec. A street vendor sold us some potatoes, which we would chop up and fry in oil. But the real problem was finding the right curds. We set out into the markets of Zanzibar looking for any type of cheese that would even come close. Nothing. Every street vendor was left confused by our description of the cheese we were looking for. Finally, we headed to a tourist area and spotted a South African–owned specialty food shop; inside, we came across a small brick of tasteless white cheddar kept in a chiller. The price was exorbitant, but it was the best we'd find. We carved the cheese into small chunks, as curd-like as we could make them. It was far from perfect, but it was still a small taste of home on the African savannah.

While that African poutine was delicious, even if it was geographically incongruous in Tanzania, it showed the limitations of any possible global spread for poutine. The cheese curds that are essential in poutine don't really travel well.

Two things have now become clear after my time in the Jucep with my dad: we need to go to the other possible home of poutine in Warwick, and I need to learn more about cheese curds. While some of the Roy Jucep's patrons may have disagreed about where to find the best poutine and where the dish originated, no one disagreed about the importance of cheese curds. They absolutely loved the cheese, with many customers paying extra to turn already impressive heaps of curds into small mountains.

"I knew the cheese would be important," I tell my dad as we head out of Drummondville and back into the green fields of rural Quebec. His link to cheese was the key element that started this project. "But I hadn't anticipated how important. It seems like cheese curds really could be the secret to understanding poutine and why it emerged in this small corner of Quebec in the 1960s."

He's quiet for a few beats, keeping his eyes on the road as cars drive past. "That could be it. Think about what you need for a poutine. We've always had fries in Quebec. Gravy isn't very challenging. But cheese is the missing part. It must have something to do with the cheese," he says. "There were a lot of curds in this area during those times when Mr. Roy was around. I know that. I was staying up late to make those curds with the day's fresh milk." His hands go through the motions of making curds as he grasps the steering wheel, the muscle memory still there decades later.

On either side of the road, amid the silos and family farms, cows are munching on tall grass every few kilometres as we drive. These ruminants are the tip of a bovine iceberg. Vast herds of cows are kept out of sight, remaining indoors year-round across the region. As green as it seems, this landscape is artificial, built on supply management rules from the federal government. This is the beating heart of Canada's dairy industry. Nearly half of Canada's milk is produced in Quebec, and this region is the centre of it.

As I watch dairy cows graze, contemplating the cheese curds in my future, my father has a suggestion: "You know, before we go to Warwick, we could call an old neighbour of mine from when I was a kid. He had a lot of cows, and I think he got into the cheese business." After a quick Google search, I find him in the local phone book and, before long, I'm on a call with Alain Hébert. Whereas my father left his family's dairy farm to pick up welding, Hébert stayed behind and has been making cheese his entire life. He's now retired and has time to see us at the Fromagerie l'Ancêtre, the cheese shop he cofounded and ran for nearly a decade.

We're already driving in the right direction, so we head toward Bécancour, back up Highway 55. The city itself is a collection of villages and a fast-growing industrial park. The cheese shop is far from any discernible downtown; instead, it's on a busy highway exit near a wrecking yard and a large farmers' market. The building is a modern factory, but the front of it, with a cheese shop open to the public, has been dressed up to look like a large brown barn.

When we enter Fromagerie l'Ancêtre, Hébert is sitting at a table, surrounded by small bags of cheese curds. Despite having worked as a farmer his entire life, he doesn't have a weathered face. He's trim, with dark caterpillar eyebrows that move under a tidy baseball cap as he talks. He bounds over with a big smile and squeezes my hand. "Laurent Lamothe's son speaks English and he's a writer? Wow," he says. The man is instantly likeable. Hébert and my father have known each other since they were children but haven't spoken in years. We're a long way from the old rural roads of their youth. They sit down and start bantering as I take out my pen and notebook. I'd jotted down a few questions on the way here that expose my ignorance about how milk becomes cheese. Hébert is happy to explain.

"It's really the cheese curds that make the poutine," he says. The story he begins to tell makes it clear we're in the right place. "Sometimes we don't have cheese curds here and I'll grab a firm cheddar to make poutine. It just doesn't work. The cheese melts all over the place. You really need curds. The secret about cheese curds is that they get warm but they don't melt. There's really something special about fresh curds," he continues. While my dad isn't directly interjecting, he's resumed his role as an enthusiastic supporter of our interview subject, nodding along and punctuating the other man's sentences with "*C'est ça!*"

We've taken our seats at a table in the front of the cheese shop with three steaming cups of coffee. Customers come in and out as we talk, the place doing brisk trade. The space is dominated by big coolers and an enormous variety of cheeses and butter, along with many types of curds in bags ready to be snapped up. What catches my eye in the shop are all the awards scattered around. The best Swiss Emmenthal and old cheddar at the British Empire Cheese Show, and other plaques and trophies from global cheese competitions. There's also a gold medal for the best fresh cheese curds—that one is pretty topical.

Poutine lesson number one from Hébert: if the cheese is melting all over your fork as you eat it, it's a bad poutine. "I've been in Western Canada and had the poutines over there. It's mostly frozen curds, sometimes shredded cheddar, and it just isn't the same thing." He shakes his head at the thought—a pattern is really starting to emerge about how French Canadians view poutine in the rest of Canada.

Hébert explains that curds, often called *fromage en crottes* in Quebec—literally cheese droppings—appear in one of the first stages as milk is made into cheese. "Cheese curds could be viewed as a mistake. It's really a white cheddar that has been yanked out of the process far too early," he says. Cheese curds are plucked out of the production line after only a few hours, instead of the months or years a proper cheddar would require.

Hébert speaks slowly, choosing his words carefully as he explains what's happening. "It's a simple process," he tells me. When milk curdles, it's cut into bite-sized pieces that are heated to become the squeaky cheese that tops poutine. Curds could come from other cheeses, but cheddar is best. The curds have a very mild flavour but are heavily salted. They are barely more than curdled milk at this point, and practically the only place in the world where cheese curds became popular as a snack was Quebec.

Within the admittedly small world of cheese curds, Quebec's curds are also different. They are large, calorie-dense chunks, not the small bits favoured elsewhere. Bags of curds like the ones crowding the store displays around Hébert have been popular in Quebec as far back as the 1950s, if not earlier. While some factories in French-speaking parts of Ontario and Manitoba turn out curds, the same omnipresent connection to curds doesn't exist. It's one of the quirks of Quebec that fresh cheese curds sweating on a gas station counter is both very normal and a good sign that you're in a well-run establishment. It's home.

"Poutine is in the veins of Quebecers," says Hébert. "Most families have poutine at least once a week. I'm sixty-three and I've been eating poutine for at least forty years. It's easy. Fries, sauce and cheese. You can serve it fast, and Quebec has all the ingredients locally. Every small town in the province has a place that serves its own poutine. It's junk food. That's what poutine is, and all junk food is pretty good."

A nearby school board had ordered an end to the sale of poutine in its schools earlier in the week, and Hébert has the news on his mind. He supports the move—kids shouldn't be eating too much unhealthy food, he says. But kids are also pretty crafty. "There's a snack bar that serves good poutines near most schools in Quebec. In my village, they took it out of the schools, but there's a sports centre a few hundred feet away and they now sell fifty poutines every lunch to students." He smiles, with a "what can you do about it" look on his face. My dad nods: Quebec kids will always find poutine. Nutritionists might not like it, but poutine isn't going anywhere.

The one major exception to Quebec's curd hegemony is the cheesy American state of Wisconsin, where a curd industry has been thriving for decades. In grand American fashion, the state has a self-appointed "world famous cheese curd capital" in the small village of Ellsworth. Local factories supply curds across the US, with refrigerated bags available at many Whole Foods stores. The Wisconsin village also hosts an annual curd festival.

Despite the shared love of cheese curds, there are some serious cultural differences south of the border. Quebec *fromageries* don't typically offer Cajun or taco-flavoured cheese curds like some American brands, although that is slowly starting to change. Canadians also rarely boast that you can freeze the bags of curds to make them last longer (cue the horror of Quebec cheese merchants like Hébert).

Under Quebec law, curds can only be kept on a store counter or at room temperature for one day. After twenty-four hours, they need to be moved to a refrigerator. That's when they start going from fresh and vibrant to stale. "Our money comes when they are fresh. That's when we really want to sell them. The value goes down a lot after those first twenty-four hours," Hébert explains.

Making curds is a tough business. Over the past fifty years, most of Quebec's *fromageries* have disappeared as the dairy sector underwent wave after wave of corporate consolidation. The small, local *fromagerie* that existed in nearly every Quebec village before the 1980s has largely disappeared. The *fromagerie* I'm sitting in is an obvious exception. Large multinational firms have closed many of the smaller, less efficient facilities. There are now only a few dozen *fromageries* in Quebec that still produce curds. Even big domestic operators like the province's main dairy co-operative, Agropur—which owns a staggeringly large constellation of dairy brands—have largely pulled out of the difficult curd market. Thankfully, though, there has been a resurgence in recent years. A number of local *fromageries* focused on cheese curds have opened, and rapid expansion plans are being dreamt up by some of the small but fast-growing operators. While dairy giants like Agropur or Saputo don't see much profit in the logistically intensive curd, small operators have found a niche in Quebecers who are willing to pay top dollar for a fresh bag of the stuff.

Boivin, a cheesemaker from Quebec's northern Saguenay–Lac-Saint-Jean region, is one of the upstarts that has burst onto the scene in recent years. It has turned the old paradigm of cheese coming from a nearby *fromagerie* on its head. To make it all work, it has effectively become a logistics company that also makes cheese. It has invested in machines that do most of the work, cutting and weighing cheese precisely to ensure no waste and maximum speed. It's far more profitable to make lots of curds in one place and ship them efficiently throughout Quebec. While it might feel local, it isn't. People from across the province, including far to the south in Montreal, don't know that the fresh cheese curds they are picking up as an impulse buy at the supermarket checkout line started the day hours before dawn and hundreds of kilometres to the north.

"When you're delivering cheese from Lac-Saint-Jean to Montreal in the same day, you've got a good distribution system. Cheese curds are all about the logistics now," says Hébert. "Boivin bought a local *fromagerie* a few years ago and they stopped making cheese curds here. We're in the middle of Quebec's dairy region, and at many places locally their cheese curds come all the way from Lac-Saint-Jean. It's weird to see it."

Fromagerie l'Ancêtre, which takes pride in making its own, was founded well before the recent wave of arrivals. The *fromagerie* was opened thirty years ago by ten farmers who were upset that their organic milk wasn't being used to make organic cheese. They figured if they were going through the trouble of ensuring their cows got access to fresh grass, on top of the daily hassle of using older farming methods—the *fromagerie*'s name is a nod to their ancestors—they might as well just make the cheese themselves. Hébert was one of them. He owned a farm with seventy head of cattle outside Saint-Léonard-d'Aston, a literal stone's throw from my grandfather's long-disappeared home. Hébert sold his last cows in 2016, retiring from a life spent in the fields. He says his parents had brought him into the barn as a baby, and he'd been in there almost every day of his life since. Milk is still being made in his backyard, but he isn't running the farm anymore. For nostalgia's sake, he says, he still pops into the barn every now and then. He usually finds a receptive audience of cows.

To this day, there's a direct line between the small size of individual farms in Quebec and the rise of the humble cheese curd. Hébert and the other farmers in this area are just a small part of Quebec's massive dairy industry. The province has over 10,300 dairy farms that produce nearly nine million litres of milk daily. That's nearly four swimming pools' worth of milk being produced every hour of the day, every day of the year. While it doesn't dominate the province's countryside like it once did, the dairy sector still employs tens of thousands of Quebecers. Unlike the sprawling farms across the western US, which often have herds numbering in the thousands, the average Quebec farm only has about seventy cows. The result is a dairy industry with massive political clout in Ottawa that can carpet the country's airwaves with advertising but, at the individual farm level, still looks like a cottage industry dominated by family farms.

Hébert gets up to chat with one of the managers who wants a word. "So how do the two of you know each other?" I ask my dad.

"We were neighbours. But he's younger so we didn't play much as kids. I mostly know him because his mother was my teacher at the schoolhouse," he answers.

"Oh, did you like her as a teacher?" I ask.

There's a very long pause. "She was a stern woman at school. You didn't want to cross her. But I used to sometimes do odd jobs in their barn, and at home she was very sweet. She was completely different."

Hébert sits down again and I ask him why curds are so popular.

"While *le fromage en grains* is part of our cheese culture today, they aren't—hmm, how do I say this?—flashy. They don't often win awards," he explains, using another common name for cheese curds.

I point to an award behind him. "Yes, that's a new one," he says happily.

Curds initially grew out of necessity, not the public's taste for fresh cheddar curds. In the years after World War I, the little *fromageries* dotting the province faced intense pressure to make money quickly. The small farms that sent their milk to those *fromageries* every day faced even more intense cash pressures and demanded immediate payment. This is when curds found their moment. Without much money on hand, owners of the small *fromageries* would use half the milk they were purchasing to make inexpensive curds immediately and keep the other half to make more expensive cheddar they could sell later.

"These were cash-and-carry operations. Money was tight, financing was harder to get and they didn't have time to wait months or years to get paid. So a lot of places, including me, figured the only way to get through was to make cheese that sold that day. Quebecers developed a taste for fresh cheese, and that's stayed with us through to today," Hébert adds.

"It's part of our French heritage," my father says.

Hébert nods approvingly. "A fancier cheddar like Monterey Jack, something that's more popular in Western Canada, was never that popular in Quebec. We were just too poor for it. Family farms were struggling, barely getting by."

The extreme perishability of cheese curds is a problem now for growing poutine chains, but decades ago it was a blessing for farmers and small, rural businesses.

"Cheese curds are not an easy industry, but what's nice about it is you get paid immediately," Hébert emphasizes. He leans over and points at one of l'Ancêtre's fancier cheeses. It's in a nearby open-top chiller with a number of award stickers stuck to it. "My little cheddar over there was produced five years ago. When we make a cheese like that, it will take us at least five years to get paid for our work. A cheese we're making today might not make money for a decade. But a curd gets you paid tomorrow."

To meet the schedule for curds, a *fromagerie*'s production usually starts in the hours before midnight with a batch of fresh milk, and by 3 a.m. the curds are out for distribution and the entire process is over. To make the curds, milk is heated, then salted and coagulated up to four times until it's the right firmness. The resulting curds are then cut, cooked, drained and often salted again—the salt helps keep them fresh. It takes about four hours per batch. The curds are then bagged and rushed to a truck destined for a local, or far away, market. Many *fromageries* aim to have their curds ready as close to 12:01 a.m. as possible. You don't want them to be bagged a minute earlier because the clock starts ticking on that twenty-four-hour expiration window the moment the curds are done. A minute after midnight gives you a full day to transport and sell them.

"It's a day-to-day business. The cheese is dropped in stores by 6 a.m. Because it's daily, it's really difficult to sell curds outside Quebec," Hébert says. He's tried to make it work, but the transportation is a nightmare and the appetite just isn't there. "It's fresh cheese and it's a war of distribution. When you do it well, you win. When you don't, you end up putting your unsold cheese in the refrigerator at the end of the day and selling it cheap. The good *fromageries* right now are winning the distribution war."

While it makes some cheese curds for locals, l'Ancêtre's attempts to sell into Montreal have been complicated by the difficulty in finding employees who want to work that overnight shift. Most of its cheese now goes to Western Canada, but little of it is curds. Instead, l'Ancêtre largely sells organic cheddars that take years to age. The *fromagerie* does send a pallet of curds to Toronto every few weeks, to supply the restaurants in that sprawling city that specialize in organic food and serve poutine—but those are frozen, not fresh. Otherwise, English Canada has yet to develop much of a taste for its curds.

In Quebec's dairy belt, that taste goes incredibly deep. It's not just about going to the store to buy curds—many farmers make their own. "Many of my friends and neighbours have little cheese basins. On nearly every rural road in Quebec, at least one farmer will make his own curds. Every two or three months they will throw cheese parties," Hébert says with a wide grin. "A buddy of mine just had a poutine party for about fifty people. You get out a fryer, a big vat of gravy and you make a bunch of curds. It's very simple. Everyone grabs a handful of fries and cheese, then you add as much sauce as you'd like. It's really a nice custom that exists in rural Quebec."

This rural tradition is in a bit of a legal grey area. Quebec's agricultural ministry won't allow farmers or anyone else to sell or buy homemade cheese curds, so a party where the host gives them away to friends is technically within the law. But it doesn't stop there. Underground networks of people selling cheese curds made from unpasteurized milk do exist, according to Hébert. But that's a risky business. Anyone who gets sick and shows up in hospital after consuming illicit cheese would likely find an inspector from the agricultural ministry outside their hospital room. It isn't quite fear that slips into Hébert's voice but an understanding that this outcome would be very bad indeed. A violently upset stomach caused by a shoddily made cheese would be the least of someone's problems. MAPAQ, as the agriculture ministry is known, doesn't mess around. That dreaded acronym comes up a lot in rural Quebec, and it's never said lovingly. "They will come down on you hard if you ever do something like selling homemade curds," Hébert says.

If poverty is one of the explanations for curds, and eventually poutine, why did it only happen in Quebec? Large parts of Canada have been dominated by poor farmers struggling to make ends meet throughout the country's history. And while Quebec has a large dairy industry, nearly two-thirds of Canada's cows are outside the province. The answer to that question, according to Hébert, is a now-obsolete rule that existed for decades under Canada's system of dairy price control known as supply management.

In short, under the sixty-year-old system, farmers are limited in how much milk they can produce annually to a level near what Canadians are expected to consume in the coming year. Supply management used to treat milk separately, paying more for milk that was prepared for drinking and less for "industrial milk" that would go into cheese. In Ontario and Western Canada, farmers weren't interested in making cheaper industrial milk and focused on drinking milk. To this day, according to Hébert, the more limited cheese options in English Canada can be linked to those choices decades ago. Quebec farmers didn't have the option. The province's dairy farmers were concentrated in a small area, creating a local glut of milk. Many dairy producers who would have otherwise liked to produce the more expensive drinking milk couldn't find any takers locally. That meant they had to sell to their local *fromagerie*, which turned the cheaper milk into cheese curds.

The system fell apart in the 1980s as technology improved and farmers weren't interested in selling off milk for cheap anymore. But by then the curd addiction had taken root—Quebec had been awash in cheap milk and cheese curds for decades. "I think that's Quebec's secret for poutine," says Hébert. "We had all these small farms, with all those small *fromageries* competing and using the cheaper milk. That's what gave us curds and poutine."

We've been speaking for nearly an hour and have comprehensively covered the history of local cheese curds. I spend a few minutes jotting down notes from our conversation while my dad and Hébert quickly catch up. I smile as I hear some of the banter—after so long away from Quebec and so much time planning this trip, there's something comfortable about being here. My reverie is broken when my dad stands up and says it's time to go. I thank Hébert for his time and he promises to stay in touch.

"If cheese is the reason for Quebec's poutine, let's go to the source," I say to my dad once we're back in his car. "It's time to go to a dairy farm."

He nods. "Yes, but that will have to wait," he answers. With the sun dipping lower on the horizon and his house just across the bridge in Trois-Rivières, we call time on a first successful day of driving. So far we've enjoyed one excellent poutine and have charted an expanding road map ahead of us.

Returning to my dad's house on the outskirts of Trois-Rivières, I see a "for sale" sign in the yard when we pull into the driveway. I hadn't noticed the sign in the morning when we left, but he'd mentioned his interest in selling in the past so it wasn't a complete surprise. "You're finally going to sell?" I ask him.

He puts the car in park. "The house is just too much for me now. Cutting the grass, clearing the snow, and all those empty rooms. Some of my pals have apartments not far away. I'd like that, I think," he says. We head inside to go hunting for supper.

I have decidedly mixed feelings about the house on Boulevard Saint-Jean. My first bedroom was at the end of a long hallway. It had baby blue and yellow walls, with a Montreal Expos pennant hanging above my bed. I spent countless hours in that room reading as I grew up, but it was also where I hid when my parents argued. I have fond memories of watching baseball games in the basement with my dad, but that was also where he kept his beer fridge. Often, in a herculean feat of drinking, he'd empty the entire refrigerator in a weekend. In retrospect, I was lucky in a way, as he never became aggressive as the stack of empty bottles grew beside him—he just got quiet and slowly disappeared from my childhood, leaving my mom with more work. Eventually, the family broke up and we left with mom.

After that, the house slowly stopped being my home. My dad stopped drinking but we saw him infrequently. He moved into my childhood bedroom. My stuff disappeared, and very quickly those memories from my early years disappeared with it. Over the past decade, I'd only slept in the house twice, and both times I was kept awake by the rattle of big trucks on Highway 55, which runs right behind the house.

"Have you had any offers yet?" I ask. When I watch old family videos—bright, grainy films of me or my sister as children—the feelings and nostalgia hit with full atomic strength. I don't really feel any of that right now, talking about the house.

"One guy. He offered me $125,000. He says he's a mechanic and wants my big garage in the back to work on taxis. He even wants to buy some of my big presses and welding equipment," he says. Seeing me about to congratulate him, he holds his hand up. "But one of my friends knows this guy and says he's a deadbeat, that he'll never have the down payment. He's been telling me for weeks now that he's trying to get the papers together for the bank. I don't think he's very serious."

This is the longest stretch of time I've spent with my dad since that day a few years earlier when we first decided to undertake this adventure. Later in the evening, alone with my thoughts while the house is quiet around me, I find myself suddenly surprised by a wave of sadness over the possible sale. I try to distract myself with a joke about the incredible affordability of Trois-Rivières real estate—the dream of the affordable 1990s is alive and well here!—but that won't do. I'm sad because I'm going to be losing one of the links that holds us together and, more to the point, my dad is getting old. He's aged visibly since I left Quebec. His already unsteady gait has turned into a shuffle, he's a little hard of hearing, and I noticed over the course of the day that he missed a few small details here and there. I vow to make him walk to Tim Hortons in the morning. It's only a quarter kilometre from his front door—an easy bit of exercise with a treat at the end. I fall asleep having completely forgotten about poutine.

I wake up as the sun streams into the guest room window and get ready for the day. My dad is sitting at the breakfast bar reading that morning's copy of *Le Journal de Montréal* when I make my way to the kitchen.

"Put on your shoes. Let's walk to the Tims to get the coffee this morning," I tell my dad.

"Why? You don't want to drive?" He eyes me with suspicion.

"We're going to spend the whole day in the car, and it'll be good for you," I tell him. He grumbles a bit but walks over to the front of the house and pulls on his shoes. This is about the point when I realize I'm trying to parent my parent.

Before I can think more about the oddness of aging, we're at the end of his driveway. He turns to me: "Are you sure you don't want to drive?" I tilt my head and we push on. Only 245 more metres to go.

"You know, I was thinking about it, and I'm a bit sad you're going to sell the house," I tell him.

He doesn't speak for a few steps, and his voice is serious when he responds. "Me too." He looks at me. "I have a lot of memories in that house."

Before leaving l'Ancêtre the previous day, I'd gotten a name from Hébert for a farmer we could drop in on, one of the other founders of the *fromagerie*. It only took a quick call to set things up. An hour after we'd gotten our coffee, my father and I pull into the driveway outside Louis Fleurent's house. He's a sixth-generation farmer who owns and operates a farm outside Nicolet, Quebec.

"You want to talk about poutine?" he asks, beckoning us to follow him. Unlike Hébert the previous day, Fleurent looks like a Canadian farmer out of central casting. He's wearing a checked shirt under his rain jacket, and a weather-beaten baseball cap covers his hair, which is greying at the edges. As we talk, Fleurent guides us into one of his paddocks through a light rain that has started falling. The area is covered in a dark, vibrant green of thick grass. A few of Fleurent's seventy cows come up and surround us. They are curious and start licking our raincoats. "They are unusually affectionate this morning," he says. More cows come over as interest spreads through the herd—if you've never been surrounded by dozens of sodden dairy cows, with pairs of brown eyes piercing through moppy heads of hair, it's a nearly indescribable place of zen, possible trampling and wholesome nosiness.

I mention that we didn't see many cows out this morning on neighbouring farms. "That's right," the farmer explains. "We're certified organic. That means the cows need to spend a certain amount of time roaming out in the paddocks, eating real grass. They spend a lot of time outside."

That makes life on the farm more complicated and more interesting. Fleurent really needs to know his cows. Most dairy cows in Canada are kept indoors most, if not all, of the time. They are closely monitored to maximize how much milk they produce. "You won't see a lot of cows out in the fields around here," he says with irritation, looking around at his neighbours' farms. He's taken a harder route, but it does have some payoffs. As the cows circle us, Fleurent laughs as they start licking my dad's rain jacket. "They like the rain so much and are in such a good mood that we'll probably see a small production bump this morning when they go in for milking," he says.

Fleurent got into the organic game because of his love for the land. As he explains, he uses older farming methods to protect the soil so he can leave for his son and grandchildren what his father left for him. His son is planning to take over the farm in a few months. Organic milk doesn't have a significantly different nutritional value from the standard stuff. The difference is in the lives of the cows themselves; they spend lots of time outside and aren't given antibiotics unless they get sick. I haven't purchased organic milk—it's hard to understand the value of the higher price when you're standing in front of a dairy cooler—but watching these cows frolicking, I can better grasp the attraction.

The farm has a mixture of new, modern buildings and older barns. We've retreated to a barn as the rain starts coming down more steadily. Some cows follow us out of the rain. A few stragglers head off to munch on some thick grass. Fleurent explains that he sometimes joins the rural cheese curd parties thrown by his neighbours, repeating much of the story we heard from Hébert the previous day. "I've got a friend who comes over from time to time, and he makes wonderful curds on the farm from the fresh milk. I made a birthday poutine for my partner a few years ago, mostly with ingredients sourced from his farm. It was the best I've ever had," he says. "Poutine is part of our traditions now. My thought is that if you're going to eat one, eat a good one."

Hébert comes into the barn and greets us all. His friend had told him we were coming by and he decided to drop in. He smiles and tells me that after our conversation yesterday, he went home and didn't have to think about what he wanted to eat that evening. "I made a poutine! I really couldn't resist after we talked about it for so long," he says.

Standing here surrounded by wooden walls and tall piles of hay, it's easy to set my mind back fifty years to when Jean-Paul Roy was making his first poutines in Drummondville. But was Roy truly first? I'd heard a lot of enthusiasm for the claim and seen the certificate on the wall, but we needed to look into the other main contender for the title. It was time to get on with the journey and find out. We thank the two men, and my father puts his Ford into drive. I offer to take a turn at the wheel, but he wants to enjoy these old roads. Warwick is nearly an hour away, down Highway 55.

CHAPTER THREE

Warwick and the prince of poutine

"IT WAS PHYSICAL WORK MAKING CHEESE CURDS," MY DAD SAYS AS his car weaves around dairy farms on the outskirts of Warwick. "I'd work in the evening and we'd take these big forty-pound blocks of fresh cheese, nearly still milk at that point, and run them through a large cutting machine. It looked a lot like a push mower for the grass. And you'd get all these cheese curds coming out the other end..."

Once again, he is going through the stories he shared with me that started us on this journey. It was the early 1960s and he was working in a *fromagerie* in his hometown of Saint-Léonard-d'Aston, a small village midway between Trois-Rivières and Drummondville. Jean-Paul Roy was only months away from spilling gravy on a mix of fries and curds in Drummondville.

On the way here we'd sped past his village and the fields where my ancestors had tilled the soil for generations. "You know, those cheese curds we made all those years ago could have had an impact on poutine's history. Maybe even in Warwick," he tells me. "And they were the Cadillac of cheese curds," he says with a sigh.

"Nothing is quite as good as the cheese we used to take out of the basin at the factory," he continues. "It was still hot. We'd just put some salt on it, and there was milk still in the middle of the curd. It doesn't get any better. Sometimes a guy would go out and get a big bag of Dulac chips and a two-litre bottle of Pepsi and we'd have a really nice snack."

This catches me by surprise. "After work?" I ask.

"No, no, on the job. The cheese was free for us. Why wouldn't we eat it? It was good for us, and we wouldn't be hungry when suppertime came around. It saved my parents some money."

In today's era, where people are warned about time theft for even looking at their social media accounts while on the job, this seems like a throwback to a different age.

"Were you supposed to be grazing while you worked?" I ask him.

"You put your hand into the basin and took out a curd while you worked. We were making it. Who would know?"

He smiles as we drive on. He did that job decades ago, but it's still fresh to him. "Those are nice memories," he says.

Warwick takes its cheese seriously—that much is immediately clear as we get closer. It isn't just the dairy farms or the self-declared status of this town as the "Quebec capital of fine cheeses." There's also a large *fromagerie* and a few artisanal cheesemakers on the side of the road. All of it is topped off with a strong dose of weathered rural charm, with a sugar shack and an old wooden covered bridge on the edge of town. With the promise of wheels of roquefort and lemeric cheese, we're a world away from the industrial hum of Drummondville and our previous day of driving. This feels like a Quebec village dipped into a vat of New England quaintness. Could this really be where poutine started?

On paper, Warwick isn't as good a candidate as yesterday's city. Drummondville is a large and growing industrial centre, with ten times the population and a constant flow of traffic. It's conveniently located at the midway point between Montreal and Quebec City on the Trans-Canada Highway. Warwick has none of that. The entire town is less than a dozen blocks long and has a population of fewer than five thousand. Plus, it's down a sleepy road, and time seems to move slower. While the Roy Jucep in Drummondville might get more attention and patrons, Warwick locals remain convinced that this small town is where poutine was born. Unfortunately, we're about to learn that very little of that history still exists.

As we drive into town, the Cantine W catches our eye. It's one of the few restaurants operating and looks like a good place to find a dash of local poutine heritage.

With its red-paint exterior and a busy parking lot, the restaurant's history is baked into its unassuming facade. It's the kind of roadside establishment I've been looking forward to finding on this drive. There's ample seating outside and we spot a nice place to eat. Standing behind the counter, Virginie Gadbois introduces herself as the owner. She's only twenty-two and has been running the place solo for the past year. With her hair pulled neatly back into a bun, Gadbois has a warm smile. She has the friendly manner of a kindergarten teacher, but she also looks very much at home behind her poutine counter.

When I tell her the purpose of our trip—to find the home of poutine—she's quick to tell us we're in the right place. "It's from Warwick! Poutine was invented here, and we have the best poutine," she says. It's the Poutine Oath, I think to myself. People around here should get it tattooed on their bodies.

Gadbois starts telling us her story. She took over the Cantine W after her father's death a year earlier. Keeping the place open is a way for her to keep his memory going. "It was so important to him," she says. There's a photograph of her father, with a bodybuilder's physique, by the till. The Cantine W is only open during the summer months, largely serving poutine and ice cream to locals. There's a sign outside proclaiming that it has over fifty kinds of ice cream. I'm about to learn that it might have even more kinds of poutine.

Unlike most Quebec fry shacks that stick to two or three classic recipes, Gadbois serves a vast array of generously portioned dishes. She has dozens of different types of poutines on offer. I record her describing all of the poutines and it runs for several minutes. She's smiling the entire time: "We've got the Italian, Chinese, Expo, Sausage, Bacon, Duboss, Delaboss, Desrocher..." But her bestseller this summer is a special that has chicken wing sauce and pita meat on top of a regular poutine. "People really like it!" she says.

Gadbois's effervescence gives life to the somewhat somnolent town around her, and she immediately throws herself into helping us with our poutine journey. I'm here for stories about Warwick and possible directions to other places we should go in town, but she's here to ensure we eat. She immediately starts pointing at her menu and what we need to try. She's absolutely not going to let us leave without some poutine.

"Do you know much about the history of poutine in Warwick?" I ask, interrupting her cheerful persuasion.

"I know that Mr. Lachance started poutine here with a restaurant in town," she says, repeating the name that Yolande Morissette gave us back at the Roy Jucep in Drummondville. She doesn't know the specifics of that history, but what she lacks in detail, she makes up for with her wide menu of possible poutine permutations. My dad is loving the energy. I can't really get another question in.

"We're constantly testing new varieties," she tells us. "Today we're trying out a Mexican poutine, with ground beef, bacon and onions." I'm also drawn to the *méchoui* poutine, which has cheese curds and pieces of spit-roasted lamb. This is no menu for a traditionalist, and while I'm skeptical, that skepticism withers in the face of her cheer.

Gadbois tells us she'll bring out two of her bestsellers with the chicken wing sauce.

"That sounds good to me," my dad finally chimes in.

"The smallest size you've got," I request. The day is young and I want to keep room for more poutine. We have no idea what to expect.

A handful of picnic tables are stationed outside, as well as a few patio gliders—a piece of furniture I've never seen anywhere but Quebec. It's usually made of two metal benches facing each other, with a table between them and a canopy above, and the whole contraption is then attached to a platform that glides back and forth. They are essential in many of the province's backyards. While relaxing, they can be intimidating for the uninitiated. The first time my wife approached one, it was like watching an ancient Roman get on an escalator.

Sitting at the glider, we hear cicadas chirping and see heat shimmering in the distance. This is going to be a very hot day. A few minutes later, Gadbois comes out with two heaping clamshell containers the size of my arm. "This size is off-menu," she tells us. "We don't usually serve them this small. The baby size is about twice as large. We take poutine seriously." Smiling over her shoulder as she walks off, she adds, "Don't forget the Cantine W!"

The serving size is intimidating, and the whole thing is a shade of bright orange reminiscent of a pumpkin. Despite all that, it looks and smells delicious. The curds are fresh and glistening as they warm in the heat of the day. The pita meat turns out to be pork, which has been thinly sliced off a shawarma machine. The outside of the meat is crispy, while the inside remains tender. The curds and meat are piled on thick, steaming and drowning in the orange hot wing sauce that has been substituted for the regular gravy. Gadbois's fries are prepared in the classic Quebec style: thickly cut and fried in a vat of oil.

My fork dives in and, with some effort, I come out with a full load. While it's distinctly a poutine, it's unlike any I've had before. The hot sauce gives the dish an unexpected kick of heat, but the biggest challenge is the heft of each forkful. The cheese, meat and fries are substantial. I look across at my father and spot a patch of sweat forming on his temple. "She's good," he says with a thumbs-up.

After a few more bites I'm stuffed, and my dad is as well. We've been bested by poutines significantly smaller than what the locals consider the baby size. "Wow! Well we certainly ate those poutines yesterday," we tell each other at almost the exact same time. We both try not to look down at our unfinished work. Welcome to Warwick. In the poutine rivalry with Drummondville, the local weapon is abundance.

We sit at the glider a little longer with our half-eaten poutines, the clamshells flapping in the light breeze, seemingly mocking our failure to finish them off. It's my time to tell a story, and I begin to lead my dad through what I learned from prior research about the small town we're visiting.

Warwick's claim to poutine follows the story of Fernand Lachance. A former construction worker, he operated a small restaurant in the village's centre during the 1950s. Initially called Le Café Idéal, the restaurant was later renamed Le Lutin Qui Rit—the Laughing Elf. In a photo from the time, the restaurant is on the first floor of an old two-storey building covered in wood siding. There's a Coca-Cola sign hanging in the front window and an ancient car parked out front. The photo is sepia but it's clearly not the result of a modern filter, just old equipment. It's taken only a few years before some of the pictures hanging in the Roy Jucep in Drummondville, but Le Café Idéal looks decades older.

Speaking with the CBC a few months before his death in the early 2000s, Lachance said he was confident that poutine was invented at his old restaurant. The way he tells it, it was a fall day in 1957 and a regular customer, Eddy Lainesse, had a craving for french fries and cheese curds together. "He said, 'Can you put that together in a bag for me?' I said, 'Yes, I'll put it in a brown sandwich bag, but it'll make *une maudite poutine*,' a bloody mess," Lachance remembered with a laugh in the radio documentary. He sold the mix for twenty-five cents. "That's how it happened. We would shake the bag, the cheese would melt and it would make a good poutine." I'm not sure why he described the cheese as melting, and the oddness of it wasn't commented on in the reporting—Lachance wouldn't have used anything other than curds. But what is clear is that his line saying it'll make a damn mess, *une maudite poutine*, is perhaps Lachance's greatest contribution to this story. That statement is now fully mythologized in Quebec as part of poutine's backstory.

Lachance was living in a seniors' home and, as you might expect, he was eating a poutine when the radio service sat down with him. "With a shock of snow-white hair and steady eyes, he looks healthy, even trim," a CBC reporter says in a steady monotone, with a bit of surprise creeping into her voice that the man in front of her doesn't have the body she expected for someone who has presumably eaten a lot of poutine over the decades of his long life. "Today he's happy, it's poutine night," the reporter continues.

Based on Lachance's story, the population of Warwick has proudly seen itself as the rightful home of poutine for decades. Many people in Quebec know the Warwick story and that "damn mess" line. However, before asking the Roy Jucep to take down its certificate, it's worth going over what Lachance described. To paraphrase: put french fries and cheese curds in a bag for me, please. He used the word poutine to describe a dry dish with only fries and cheese. Where's the gravy?

Decades after he put in that initial order for "poutine," Eddy Lainesse, whose first name is really Jean-Guy, also spoke before his death. He had been working as a truck driver travelling the roads of central Quebec. Even late in life, he was still a large man with a powerful voice. Lainesse would go on to assert for decades that he'd given Lachance the idea for what is now one of Canada's most famous dishes.

In a way, Lainesse would claim that he'd really invented poutine by asking for the two ingredients to be mixed together. He was sitting at a restaurant bar nursing a cup of coffee on the same day the CBC spoke with Lachance. They caught up with Lainesse as well, who was clearly a poutine traditionalist. "There are many different kinds of poutine now. But hamburger meat and whatnot—it's too much, it's not funny. At the beginning, it was just fries and cheese, even the sauce came later. Seven or eight years later."

As I'm relaying this information to my dad, sitting out in the sunshine in Warwick, I can see him nodding along with growing vigour. He's starting to connect the dots in my research, but honestly, the whole scope of the story is only really coming together as I say it out loud.

I continue with what I know. Le Café Idéal would eventually add gravy to its menu. Lachance's wife, Germaine, a partner at the restaurant and an accomplished cook herself, disagreed with her husband's gravy-phobic ways. She threw together a sauce that could be added to the increasingly popular poutine. However, even at the end of his life, Lachance was still enjoying his version of poutine—with fries and cheese, but no gravy. On the day of the CBC interview, he asked the cook for a little pot of sauce on the side. "But not too much sauce," he added, in some of his last words ever recorded. He died at the age of eighty-six in 2004.

I take a few moments to enjoy the warmth of the day. It's a break from driving and conversation. Then I look over and see a grin on my father's face. This quiet moment is worth remembering for him as well. After a few more deep breaths, I decide it's time to finish with the Lachance story. I ask my father a simple question: "What goes in a poutine?"

"It's fries, cheese and gravy," he tells me, tilting his head at what might seem like a silly question.

"Can you have a poutine without gravy?" I ask.

"No. I guess the gravy is actually quite important."

We both feel comfortable with this conclusion, but one additional part of the story remains unresolved, and that's in the name itself. Lachance's exclamation that he'd make a *maudite poutine* clashes with the Drummondville story that the coining of poutine came from the Ti-Pout nickname of the cook who poured on so much of that early gravy.

It does require a deep belief in coincidence to accept that two towns, a short drive from each other, would have independently come up with the exact same name for a similar dish only a few years apart. However, based on the story of a meeting of cooks and other staff in the Roy Jucep kitchen, it's possible—maybe even likely—that a member of the Roy Jucep team had heard people from Warwick use the word *poutine* or had seen it on Lachance's menu over the previous few years. Perhaps they then recalled poutine as a good name for Ti-Pout's dish when the restaurant went looking for something to replace the ponderous "cheese-fries-gravy" description. To accept that Warwick's restaurant had a significant role to play in poutine's creation, at the very least gifting us a name for the dish, doesn't undercut what was later built in Drummondville.

We get back into the car and head to the site of Le Café Idéal. There's nothing there. Lachance's restaurant closed decades ago, and while a number of businesses have since taken its physical place, none has been a poutine restaurant claiming that original lineage. The Roy Jucep's certificate seems safe, if only because few restaurants are left in Warwick to mount a challenge. The only other place in Warwick making poutine is a Fromagerie Victoria franchise that opened a few years ago. It's a chain restaurant headquartered in a nearby city. The lack of local poutine options is a significant change of fortune for a town that has a special entitlement to poutine's history.

Warwick does have an additional, more recent claim to poutine. Since 2019, the town has held the Guinness World Record for the largest serving of poutine ever dished out. Weighing in at a whopping 3,034 kilograms, the poutine was a titanic offering. To win the record, the poutine had to be a single dish made authentically; it couldn't be several helpings made separately and thrown together at the end. On the day of the record-breaking, a bespoke tray of wood and steel over eighteen metres long was constructed to hold the finished behemoth. The dish was nearly one-third cheese by weight, and both the local Fromagerie Warwick and the nearby Fromagerie Victoria factory had to be used to make enough curds—and the curds all had to have been made in the previous twenty-four hours, both legally and for taste. Over four hundred volunteers were then put to work on forty-two deep fryers for the fries, while about one thousand litres of gravy were prepared. In the end, over six thousand people were needed to eat the thing, more than the population of Warwick itself. As they ate, they were spurred on by a song composed for the occasion: the "Hymne à la Poutine." Locals remain proud of the win.

During our time in Warwick, I'm struck by how people both here and in Drummondville want to keep this rivalry going. They enjoy claiming poutine as their own, not because of the international stature of the dish today and any fame it could bring their hometowns, but because of a deep personal connection to what poutine represents. People I speak with in restaurants in both towns are genuinely surprised when I talk about poutine's growing influence, not just globally but in the rest of Canada. The thought that someone in British Columbia or Alberta might want to understand poutine's history is a revelation to many. They've kept their focus so local for so long, facing the town down the highway, that they've missed what has happened with the dish they love in the rest of the world.

While the question of who invented poutine might cause some friction in the region, the two men closest to the centre of the action kept a pretty nonchalant attitude during their lifetimes. The similarities between their duelling narratives remain notable. Not only was poutine born as a regional dish, cooked up in small towns far away from the pressure cooker of large cities where many of our other favourite foods were developed, but the closeness between the towns is remarkable. In the decades since, poutine has established deep roots across the area.

It's time to leave Warwick—poutine's cradle, if not exactly its home. As we drive north, my dad tells me a story I've never heard before. "When I was working at the *fromagerie* as a teenager, hefting all those blocks of cheese, I also took over my father's milk run. I think it was 1964," he says as he drives. That is why he's so familiar with these small roads. Not only did he drive them with his friends, but for four years he woke up early to pick up fresh milk soon after farmers had collected it. "My first client was just outside the door. It was my dad. I'd go around and load these big eight-gallon milk jugs into the back of an old truck and then drive off. The milk run paid good money," he continues. That was especially true for a twentysomething kid from a dairy farm in rural Quebec. He soon had enough money to buy a new car, one of the new American jobs with a big engine and an ocean of chrome covering the body.

It was hard work. I can see his mind turning back to all those decades ago. My dad had insisted that his own children work, and I've pretty much had a job in some form or another since I was eleven. I spent my preteen summers working in a farmer's fields to earn enough money to buy my first bicycle. "You've got to earn money for yourself and your family," my dad would always say. It's all suddenly making more sense.

"My route was made up of small farmers who had a dozen cows at most. The farmers would milk the cows by hand and had large families to help them out. There was new technology coming, but it hadn't arrived yet," he says. We drive past the silos and the barns of those same farms he once stopped at, now passed down to the grandchildren of the farmers he once knew. He stops his story to tell me their names. Decades after the farmers died, he still refers to them formally as "mister" this or that, always saying their last names with significant respect. It's a lovely glimpse of an age long gone. "All these guys were farmers, but they also had another job on the side. They worked as labourers mostly, for other farmers, or fixing roads for the highways department. They couldn't survive off the money they made from the farm alone," he tells me.

Within months of starting work on his milk run, my dad began looking like a gym regular, with enormous shoulders that he'd keep for the next half century. "It was real exercise. Each morning, I'd pack 250 jugs three-high in the wooden tray of this big, grunting GM five-ton truck," he says. The vehicle would end up suffering worse than his sore shoulders, needing weekly trips to a local mechanic to keep it running. I remember those broad shoulders and ropey forearms from my youth, but in the decades since they've faded away completely. I look at him now and there's a heavy dose of melancholy as I notice how much smaller he's gotten with age.

"I had to work fast. It took time to load the truck, and as the day went on and I drove up the dozens of driveways to each of the family farms on my milk run, the sun would be starting to warm the day. Often the farmers would come outside and tell me what milk jugs to take away. They'd keep what they needed to feed their own families." Our car is kicking up walls of dust as we pull out of a small town on our way north. "These farmers weren't rich and didn't have any money to invest in any refrigeration. Instead, they'd do what their ancestors had done and lower the bins down a deep well. The cold water would help preserve the milk." I'm caught by surprise. It makes sense, but I hadn't thought of that before.

"Did it work?" I ask him.

"Absolutely. That's what my dad did."

He explains that not only would he need to heave the jugs into the back of his truck, but he often also needed to pull them up from the depths of a well. "That's when a farmer had the time. But more often, the farmers would need to head out for the morning's work quickly, and the jugs would sit on the porch, baking in the day's sun. It didn't always make for the best quality control.

"By the time I pulled into the *fromagerie* parking lot, I'd often be carrying a full load of warm milk. The jugs were also cleaned by hand, so sometimes the farmers didn't quite get out the previous day's sticky residue. Sometimes the milk spent two hours waiting on the front step and bacteria formed. You smelled it when you opened up some jugs. If it was really bad, the *fromageries* would refuse the milk." He gives me a look of disgust—the aroma of sour milk has been living in his mind for decades.

What my dad hadn't known was that things were about to change. "*Fromageries* started demanding more from farmers. Better quality, more attention to what they were doing. Almost overnight, the order went out that farms needed to add big refrigerated tanks to their barns," he continues. The otherwise small technical tweak transformed Quebec's milk industry nearly overnight.

I think I can see where this is going: my dad's old truck and his milk jugs were immediately rendered obsolete.

There's a long pause now in his storytelling. He looks ahead to the road, ignoring me as he takes a deep breath. "That didn't necessarily need to be the end of my milk run," he goes on. "Lactantia, the big dairy co-operative, offered to buy me a big, modern truck. The kind you still see on the road today with a big stainless steel tank. They came to my dad's farm and said I was doing a good job and they wanted me to keep doing the work. I'd need to take a two-week course in Drummondville. However, I'd need to repay the co-operative for the truck and equipment. It was about $70,000. The repayment terms were generous," he remembers. "But I panicked. I'd never had that much money. $70,000! The thought of being that deep in debt, well, frankly, it terrified me. So I walked away."

There's a long silence in the car as I think about what he just said. I'd never heard any of this before. It was a golden ticket out of the life he'd been living, but he turned them down.

"You were afraid of the debt. You were young," I tell him.

"I should have done it," he says with emotion creeping into his voice. He was in his mid-twenties and the life he'd known was a manual one. He got up early, he milked his dad's cows, he drove fifty miles to the creamery, he picked up jugs along the way, he drove the fifty miles back home. It was safe, honest and unchanging work. He and his father and grandfather had lived in the same small corner of Quebec, largely living in the same way. He was used to worrying about today—he didn't often think about tomorrow.

"You'd never really thought about the future like that. You couldn't imagine what was coming next," I say, trying to soothe him. He is having none of it. He sounds gloomy and stops talking to sip his coffee. The modern world had come roaring into his world, upsetting everything he'd known in a revolution of noise and innovation. He flinched.

"So what happened next?" I ask.

"The co-operative went down the road and asked my neighbour if he'd take the same deal. He took it."

I'm confused. "So you just gave it up?" I ask.

"If I didn't want to take on the debt, it wasn't mine anymore. So I walked away from my milk run." Another long pause. "What I didn't know is that the industry was changing quickly. The small farmers who couldn't afford refrigerators sold their cows, and the farms consolidated almost overnight," he says. "Instead of all these small farms, only a few big operators were left. The drive was a fraction of what it had been. My neighbour had a new truck. I could see him get up later in the morning. He'd just back his big rig up to a few barns, plug it in and fill it up," he concludes.

"I guess no more throwing milk jugs or pulling them out of wells for him," I say.

"Not at all. He actually paid off his debt in two years, bought a second truck and had crews running both of them. Then he sold the entire thing for about $420,000 a year later." That's about $4 million in 2024 dollars. Only three years after my dad had given away the business for free.

Meanwhile, my dad went looking for another job. He tried his hand at being a mechanic but was delicately told after a few weeks that he was too slow—"*méticuleux*" was the word they'd used, he remembers. He then decided to learn to become a welder, the job he'd keep for the rest of his working life. While training for that, he learned that his milk run had been sold for a small fortune. "That choice was the biggest regret of my life, and I never really told anyone before now," he tells me.

I feel a flood of emotions as he's telling me the story. He would have had a completely different life if he'd taken the deal. He was always a kind man, but life would offer him very few breaks over the coming decades. He'd continue working hard into his seventies, trudging to northern Alberta in winter or anywhere else he could find work welding two big pipes together. But back then, in 1968, he just didn't know how much the world was changing. And it was only going to start changing faster.

After several minutes of silence as we travel down Route 116, we spot the welcome sign for Princeville. The conversation at the tourism office at the start of our journey rattles back into our minds, with Clement Prince's proud certainty that this, his hometown, was where poutine was born.

Only slightly larger than Warwick, Princeville has a familiar feel to it. There are more maple trees around, and a significant amount of local industry is turning out that other Quebec delight, maple syrup. One thing that Princeville does have going for it is a big poutine restaurant right in the centre of the village. The Princesse restaurant might not be at the top of anyone's list of poutine spots to visit, but that's only because of its relative anonymity. Prince, the helpful clerk, had mentioned that we should stop at the Princesse. It's fine advice—we need a break after our conversation.

From the outside, the Princesse restaurant appears completely unimpressive. Unusually, it looks like a suburban house from the 1980s, with vinyl siding and faux brick, with the inside of the house appearing to have been opened up quickly into a restaurant. The one thing that stands out from the drab surroundings is a red cow's head on the marquee outside, with "*fromage en grains*" in bright neon letters. The sign is a local landmark. Inside, the decor isn't much better than the unassuming facade, with inexpensive weathered tables and stacked chairs.

Despite its plain appearance, the restaurant is crowded when we walk in. There's one small table in the corner that's still free, and a busy waitress points us to it. "*Pour deux,*" she says. My excitement level just went from low to off the scale: a crowded poutine restaurant in rural

Quebec, on a secondary highway, in a small town far from a large city. This is all a powerful suggestion that something mighty good is happening inside. Thank you, Mr. Prince.

We sit down and discover that miraculously we're hungry again, as the hefty poutine from Cantine W has disappeared into a hunger vortex that only a team of astrophysicists could begin to explain.

A large man comes to drop off some menus. My dad repeats his script from the previous day: "This is my son and we're researching poutine. We're going to write about the history of it," he tells the man. I join in this time—our two-man act on the road is slowly coming together. "Do you know if someone here could talk about that?" The man nods, and it turns out he's the owner, Bruno Lamontagne.

"There's a lot of history here. The Princesse has been using the same poutine recipe for decades," he says.

"People must like it. You seem to be very busy," I tell him.

"Every day," he answers. As a proxy for how busy the restaurant is, Lamontagne tells us they use 125 kilograms of cheese curds daily—that's nearly twice as much as at the Roy Jucep. While the restaurant is somewhat more generous with the curds on each poutine, it's not that much more generous than the far better-known rival in Drummondville. The poutines are flying out of the kitchen as we chat. This place is a well-oiled assembly line.

The Princesse is a family-run restaurant and Lamontagne is its seventh owner. He's been walking the vinyl floors with plates of poutine for over three decades. Not just another typical Quebec roadside *casse-croûte*, the Princesse has a deep reservoir of history. "We were one of the first. For decades, the menu here called a poutine a '*mixte.*' You know, like a mix of ingredients. But over time we changed the name as poutine became better known," he tells us, standing as he talks.

"Is it true that the restaurant's first owner is seen by some locals as the real inventor of poutine?" I ask him.

"That's true," he says, explaining that the founder owned a nearby *fromagerie* and sold fries, gravy and bags of cheese at the Princesse. "I'm told that a man came here and asked for the restaurant to mix in sauce with his fries and cheese. He said it would make a 'poutine.' Apparently that's how it started," Lamontagne says. "But locals didn't like that name for a long time."

I'm going to be honest: his heart isn't really into telling this story. "I've told it so many times," he confirms. He doesn't have the energy of Virginie Gadbois at the Cantine W, but he's also got decades on her. He's also a bit tired after selling hundreds of plates of poutine just today. He starts tapping his foot—there are some gaps in the story and it seems likely they'll stay there. What is clear is that the Princesse called the dish a *mixte*, and while the founding details are hazy, they are nearly identical to the stories just down the road in Warwick and Drummondville. Lamontagne couldn't tell me what specific year the event is believed to have happened. Research on the town's poutine past is pretty much a dry hole, but the restaurant opened in 1967, nearly a decade after Eddy Lainesse walked up to the counter in Warwick and asked for his poutine.

"Would you like to order one now?" Lamontagne asks.

Waiting on two original poutines from the kitchen, we reflect on what we've seen over the past two days. "Do you think Warwick invented it?" my dad asks. "I didn't know all the history the town has with poutine."

I take a moment to collect my thoughts. "Mr. Lachance in Warwick invented a dish called poutine that mixed together fries and cheese curds in a brown paper bag," I begin. "Eddy Lainesse, a truck driver who often found himself in a hurry, had stumbled on a novel way of getting a quick lunch to go. It seems likely he would have started putting in his order everywhere around this small region of Quebec. He'd do so at stops in Warwick, Nicolet, Drummondville and

Victoriaville. I think he likely spread the idea until others took it up. It's clear that these two men helped set the foundation for what we know as poutine today." Glasses of water appear and I take a sip. "However, it took Jean-Paul Roy to add that critical third ingredient. A poutine, as we understand the word today, requires hot gravy. Roy was in the right place at the right time, with a great gravy recipe sitting in his back pocket—one that turned Warwick's fries and cheese into something magical. While some may have initially seen gravy as a distraction from the beauty that is cheese and fries combined, poutine needs its three main ingredients together, at a minimum. Warwick is irreplaceably important, but I just can't see it as the birthplace."

My monologue over, Lamontagne appears out of the kitchen with two poutines and heads straight for us. "Here you go," he says. The presentation is different in nearly every way from your standard poutine. For starters, all three ingredients have come separately. The fries are in the centre of the plate, the cheese curds are off to the side and the gravy is in a little bowl by itself. It's incredibly odd, especially for a place that called its poutine a *mixte* for so many years. Nothing comes mixed, with diners invited to push the ingredients together and combine them however they'd like. If I were anywhere else, I'd be skeptical about the situation, but I push that thought aside for the moment as I remember the enthusiasm of the restaurant's diners.

First, I try the elements individually. The fries are crinkle-cut, which is highly unusual for poutine. The gravy is even sweeter than the one at the Roy Jucep, which puts it very far along that end of the sauce spectrum. But as I pick up a curd, I feel like we've got a winner. The curds steal the show—they are incredibly plentiful, succulent and squeaky. The *fromagerie* that supplies them is still nearby, Lamontagne had said, and the quality is impeccable. Excited for what's to come, I mix some fries and curds together and pour gravy onto them from the bowl.

I take my first bite, then a second and third, without coming up for air. This is about as close to a perfect poutine as I've had. The ingredients mix perfectly together. Even the otherwise overly sweet sauce dances on the curds as I tuck into them with joy. I'd kept a bit of everything in reserve and proceed to mix it up quickly. Within three minutes, my plate is empty. "Wow, that's a good poutine," I tell my dad. He nods, taking his time. Before I pick up my fork and eat some fries off his plate, Lamontagne comes back over and takes a seat.

"How important is poutine to this place?" I ask.

He grunts. "Everything revolves around poutine," he says. His tone makes it clear that he means more widely than just his restaurant. "When I was growing up, I probably had my first poutine here when I was ten years old. It was a pretty rare treat, maybe something for a special Sunday. Life has changed so much these days. People eat out every Sunday now," Lamontagne tells us. The buzzing crowd moving around us continues to give proof of poutine's enduring popularity in this small corner of Quebec.

"The Princesse is the closest thing that Princeville has to its first poutine restaurant," Lamontagne says, explaining that an earlier restaurant closed in the mid-1960s, and then the Princesse we're sitting in opened in 1967. It was named after an adjoining *fromagerie*, which originally was owned by the same man. After a few sales over the years, it fell into Lamontagne's lap. "If you want to wait a bit, you can go back to the kitchen and see where it happens," he adds.

The poutine rush slows in the afternoon at the Princesse. Nathalie Bergeron is standing in the kitchen wielding a large chef's knife. She has headphones on to hear the orders coming in. She's one of the staff members who has worked here for years alongside Lamontagne. "The knife is for the cheese," she tells me, seeing me staring at her culinary broadsword.

I soon learn that her job in this kitchen is a full-body workout. "I'm preparing for the dinner rush. There's going to be a lot of poutine orders going out, and we need to get ready," she explains. She bends over and grabs a one-kilo bag of cheese curds from under the metal kitchen counter. She tosses it up and brings it smashing down onto the metal with a loud thud. "We get these beautiful curds, but sometimes they're too big," she says. Cutting the bag open, she spills the cheese out and goes to work methodically, using the dull side of her knife to break up the large curd chunks. That bag done, she grabs another. After fifteen minutes, she has several large plastic tubs full of cheese. These bins will be empty soon enough, eaten by the next crowd of patrons, even before people come in with later orders for dinner. "In this region, we've grown up on poutine. We take it very seriously," she says.

The Princesse restaurant feels like a small but charming piece of poutine's history. It's unassuming and completely lacking in pretension. From the *mixte* name on the menu to the odd crinkle-cut fries, it's a different spin on an old classic. There are few institutions left like it.

And unfortunately, the Princesse is no longer one of them. A few months after my father and I left the Princesse, I received upsetting news from Princeville. A Molotov cocktail had been tossed through one of the restaurant's windows. While the damage was severe, much of what made the Princesse special survived. Facing a $200,000 repair bill, Lamontagne and his family got to work restoring what they could. They rushed and got the restaurant reopened for the holidays, welcoming locals back on December 18. The lineup for poutine came back with a fury, the soot and smoke scrubbed away. Five days later, a few hours before Christmas Eve, the firebug struck again. This time, the Princesse was completely destroyed. Standing in front of a hole filled with snow, Lamontagne's daughter could only wonder about why the restaurant was hit not once but twice: "Is it the competition?

Is it someone alone who decided to do this? What we do see is that the Princesse restaurant was bothering someone," she said at the time.

Quebec's provincial police investigated and offered a $2,000 reward for information about the crime, but the Princesse's demise remains a mystery at the time of writing. The Lamontagnes said repeatedly that they'd received no threats or warnings before the fires. Locals were outraged by the destruction of a local institution that was a weekly, if not daily, part of many lives. The world of poutine, as full of argument and debate as it can get, doesn't usually devolve into arson.

Lamontagne chose not to rebuild in the same way. But that's not the end of the story. Instead, the Princesse headed back to its roots. A food truck called La P'tite Vache (the Small Cow), modelled on a 1960s-era *casse-croûte*, is now permanently parked on the site. In an echo of Jean-Paul Roy's original chip wagon, La P'tite Vache is now a seasonal roadside stop that serves ice cream and other treats. There are hot dogs and hamburgers, but poutine remains at the top of the menu. Now more than ever, the poutine is king in Princeville, with the food truck invoking the long history of the dish where it's parked. The neon red cow sign from the old restaurant is still there, giving its name to the food truck and serving as a north star for Princeville's locals when they're searching for poutine.

CHAPTER FOUR

The golden fork comes home

I T WAS 2011, AND SOMETHING WAS WRONG AT THE ROY JUCEP.
Charles Lambert had bought the restaurant a few months earlier
and was hearing from diners that the rich, brown sauce getting poured
onto his poutines—not just any poutines, but the dish coming out of
poutine's federally recognized home—just wasn't what it had once
been. Sometime over the decades since the restaurant's gravy was first
perfected by Jean-Paul Roy, the recipe had changed. He suspected
that in an unfortunate moment of culinary vandalism, someone had
tinkered with the spices and ratios of Roy's formula, making the once
sweet gravy much spicier. The original recipe had gone missing years
earlier, and now Lambert was getting an earful that his poutine wasn't
living up to what people remembered.

Lambert isn't a chef or a guru in the kitchen. He's a businessman
who invests in real estate and runs a taxi company in Drummondville.
While he's far more comfortable with a spreadsheet than a spatula, he
now owned the Roy Jucep and its reputation, and he understood that
he had to do something about the complaints.

And so here he was, cleaning out the restaurant's dusty back office.
Against a wall was a cupboard that hadn't been touched in years. It
was full of rusty keys that didn't open any locks or doors. Digging

through layers of administrative sediment made up of paper and junk that had accumulated over decades, he found something coated in grime. "It was a binder full of recipes, including one for a sauce," he tells me, years later. It was an old piece of paper, weathered and faded. "I went into the kitchen and showed it to the cook. She said that wasn't the recipe we use today, so I asked her to make up a batch. Yolande Morissette, she really is our local guru, she had a taste and confirmed that it was the sauce that Jean-Paul had made back in the day."

It's now our third day of driving and we've travelled back to Drummondville and the Roy Jucep. We're at the restaurant not to peer into poutine's past but to look toward its future. During our last time here, I'd heard that Lambert would want to chat with us about his plans for the restaurant. After an email, he quickly agreed. My dad took almost no convincing to make it our next stop. "Yes! That's where poutine came from and it was good poutine. Let's go," he said, grabbing his jacket and heading for the door.

We arrive at the Roy Jucep early, slip through the front door and aren't recognized by any of the staff as the two guys who'd spent hours there the day before. We put in two orders for that same authentic poutine. They arrive quickly and deliciously. Just as we finish up, I notice someone who looks like Lambert coming into the restaurant. It's time for our interview. I go up and introduce myself, and he's surprised that we'd beaten him here. Lambert is wearing a button-down shirt and dress pants. The professional look is somewhat offset by a thick mop of grey hair that spills over his ears. After a firm handshake, he tells us to follow him as he sets off for his favourite corner booth in the back. With a smile, he sets down his business card on the table in front of us. "Where do you want to start?" he asks.

In the decade since he bought the restaurant, Lambert has accidentally fallen into a role as poutine's unofficial spokesman. He soon begins telling me about the importance of the Roy Jucep's poutine

sauce. He tells me and my father that after he found that small piece
of paper with the recipe, he brought it home, scanned it and put the
digital document in a safe place.

"Have you saved it to the cloud?" I ask.

"I'm not telling you that. If I told you I'd have to kill you," he says.
It's clear he's joking, but there's no smile on his face.

He faced a dilemma after his discovery. He was, and remains,
convinced that the Roy Jucep's signature sauce is what sets its iconic
poutine apart. No one else at the restaurant knew how to make the
gravy, so he could share the recipe and risk it falling into the wrong
hands, or keep it close. Lambert, the lawyer-businessman-owner who
isn't a cook, decided it would be best if he kept it to himself.

He now produces the spice base for the gravy at his home. In
secret. He's not sharing what he knows with me or anyone else. "I mix
the spices for the sauce in my garage. I make it personally. It's a secret
recipe. The spices are ordered separately, they are delivered separately
and they aren't billed to the same place. I even order them in a completely random way to ensure no one can take the order and copy the
recipe." He's still completely serious—maybe I shouldn't be so surprised about the lengths he'll go to for poutine.

"I make it once a year, give or take. Each time I do it, the recipe
works out to about ten months' worth of sauce. We store the spices in
the basement at the restaurant here, and a camera is pointed at them
around the clock," he says. "Employees take a single package of spices
every day. Then the actual sauce is made fresh in the kitchen." Despite
all the trouble and effort he engages in to ensure people get that original
sauce, he never announced the change to the restaurant's patrons. One
day in late 2011, he swapped out the altered recipe from recent decades
and brought back the sweeter classic. He's been using it ever.since.

To understand his obsession with the sauce, Lambert says you
need to understand the context of when the Roy Jucep started. Nearly

every restaurant in the region had cheese curds back in those days. Cooks and customers would travel across Quebec, eating and working, and they'd drag tastes, ideas and recipes with them. Some were mixing fries with gravy, others were dumping cheese curds into their bags of fries. Poutine came together as a fusion of different ideas. "It's rare that a restaurateur is alone in inventing a dish. It comes together from lots of places," he says. Rather than looking at this as a battle of restaurateurs, the argument can be made that poutine's true inventor is the people of its home region, those patrons who kept ordering the messy mix decades ago.

But why did all three ingredients come together at the Roy Jucep for the first time, leading to that certificate by the door?

"It's obvious," according to Lambert, who is tilting his head. "Roy clearly had the best gravy. People today still rave about it, even after the classic recipe was restored." He wants to be clear that this isn't just good marketing—it's the gravy.

To go through all the effort of bringing back an old sauce, including clandestinely making it in his garage, you'd think Lambert would be a poutine or Roy Jucep purist. He's neither. In terms of Drummondville's population, he's in a small minority that has no deep personal relationship with the restaurant. He first stepped foot in the Jucep only two months before he bought the place. "A bunch of us were going to Montreal for the Formula One. We came here for breakfast and then all drove up in one car. I'd never been here before. I think that's proof I'm not a big poutine eater. One month later I saw an advertisement to buy this place, and a month after that I shook hands to buy it." The outgoing owner's last bit of advice was to avoid any gimmicks or promotions. "He told me, 'Just focus on making good poutine,'" Lambert says. "That's what people in Drummondville want. And so far, it's been good advice."

The Roy Jucep is now an inherently tradition-bound institution. At the top, the restaurant's ownership hasn't seen much turnover during the past half century. Lambert is only the third owner since Jean-Paul Roy parted ways with the place that bears his name. The waitstaff often stays on for years, if not decades, and the recipes are now largely frozen in time, reflective of the era that brought the eatery to glory. In other restaurants, that stasis could turn into dullness and decay, but that fate isn't visible at the Roy Jucep. Instead, it's busy and humming. The deep embrace of history isn't a sign of stagnation, it's the point: "If there's a book about poutine and we aren't in it, that's a bad book about poutine. Someone hasn't done their work. This is where it all started," says Lambert.

While he occasionally rolls up his sleeves at the restaurant, he doesn't hide the fact that buying the Roy Jucep was about profit. It's not a vanity project or a way to get himself a nicer seat on the local chamber of commerce. "I'm not a restaurateur. I would have never started a restaurant from scratch," he says. "It really was a question of numbers. I'm a businessman. It was a good opportunity."

Lambert is part of a new generation of managers, far removed from the swashbuckling early days of packed crowds and police. But along with prepping the sauce mix in his garage with a paddle, for Lambert, the Jucep hasn't been a typical business. He was warned when signing the papers to buy the place that it might come with more attention than other restaurants. *Caveat emptor.* The requests for information and interviews soon began coming in, and he learned on the fly to speak to the media. Sitting here with me and my dad, he seems pretty at ease. There are no microphones or klieg lights, so the pressure is off as I ask questions and my dad hangs back, not saying much this time.

"Poutine has really taken off around the world since I bought this place. But I think we've missed a bit of an opportunity to grow here with the labour shortages in Quebec. We've been in newspapers around the world. We even had Swiss radio set up with a Winnebago in the parking lot for three days reporting on the invention of poutine. I still have no idea what that was about," Lambert says with a laugh.

While he might not have known it at the beginning, all the attention has shifted some of his thinking. Turning a profit is still a primary goal, but he concedes that there's now a larger responsibility as well. "The Roy Jucep is a jewel, not just locally, but nationally as well. There's constant interest in poutine and where it was invented. That's why we keep our original poutine on the menu—we try a new creation every month, but we need to keep the original. In Montreal at Au Pied de Cochon they'll make you a foie gras poutine," he says, referring to one of the metropolis's top restaurants. "If we started making that, who would be left to make the real original? There wouldn't be anyone left. That's our responsibility."

My dad now pipes up. As someone whose memories of the Roy Jucep were jogged by remembering the restaurant in its heyday, when servers ran trays out to people waiting in big American cars, he wants to know more.

"You had the carhops here, right?" he says.

Lambert nods his head. "The carhop service always comes up during conversations with locals. People really liked pulling up and getting served in their cars," he says. But over time, the popularity of eating at the wheel faded. There was a last attempt to bring it back in the 1980s, but it was quickly abandoned.

"Would you consider bringing it back?" I ask.

He shakes his head.

"A previous manager told me that health and safety rules would make carhops a legal and regulatory nightmare," I say. "Is that why?" I've done my research.

Lambert continues shaking his head. He won't bring it back, and the reason is simpler than that: "People today don't want to eat in their cars. They are worried about spills and stains. Cars are a lot smaller than they were back then. Honestly, they were twice the size. Setting up with a tray of poutine and a glass of Pepsi in a small car, forget about it."

This is when Lambert reveals that there is a secret on the Roy Jucep's menu. Most diners would assume the "authentic poutine" listed on the menu is the authentic dish the inventor would have made. It's not. The authentic has the cheese on top. Three-quarters of the way down the menu is the less prominent "original poutine." That name, he explains, is literal. The original has the cheese at the bottom, under a thick bed of fries and gravy. "That's the way the Roy Jucep used to serve poutine, and it's the correct way," Lambert tells me. Future reprints of the menu will change the order of the poutines and move the original to the top, he promises.

"It was some restaurants in Quebec City that started putting the cheese on top, and then Montreal restaurants followed. When I went to study in Montreal, I didn't get why they piled all the cheese on top. You know, 'That's not how you make a poutine,' I thought at the time. But it was just to show that there was cheese in it. I'm told Mr. Roy wasn't happy at all when the Jucep eventually followed the trend. People had been complaining that the Jucep didn't put enough cheese in the poutine, so the owner before me bowed to pressure and put it on top so they could see it. Now that we finally brought the original back to the menu with the cheese on the bottom, it's staying there," he says. I make a mental note to get an original during my next swing through Drummondville.

Despite all the talk of heritage, Lambert does have wider plans to break out of the restaurant's home terrain. He'd initially planned to expand the Roy Jucep beyond its only home with a series of new locations under a Jucep Express banner. Based on Quebec's love of poutine, it seemed a great way to grow the business and sell the Jucep's invention story. But he soon ran into a problem that has faced many

Quebec entrepreneurs in recent years, especially in rural areas like Drummondville: systemic and growing labour shortages. Quebec's aging population and healthy economy have meant an explosion in help-wanted signs across the province, from Montreal to Tadoussac. "Our biggest challenge isn't getting people to come to the counter but getting them behind it," Lambert says.

Until he can expand, he's protecting what he has. Lambert recently renewed the trademark for being poutine's inventor. "It's our main way of publicity and it reinforces the belief that this is where poutine started. This is where they gave the name poutine to that mix. This is the first place a menu had the word p-o-u-t-i-n-e on it," he says, reading out each letter separately. "And this was the first place that only meant fries, cheese and sauce."

The trademark should be good for another two decades, and it won't be leaving its perch beside the Jucep's door. Well, except for the occasional theft.

Mylène Héroux, the restaurant's manager, slides into the booth beside Lambert. After three years of running the restaurant, she has the numbers at her fingertips. "We sold over sixty thousand poutines last year," she says. As you would expect, poutine makes up more than half the restaurant's sales. To keep the poutine machine running, the kitchen burns through about seventy kilograms of curds daily. On weekends or during a particularly busy day, someone in the kitchen might have to get on the phone and ask a local *fromagerie* to send over emergency deliveries of cheese. The fries come from Baril, a producer in nearby Saint-Léonard-d'Aston, my father's birthplace. Everything is local, fresh and comparatively inexpensive, she says.

One of the perks of Héroux's job is to help plan a monthly special poutine—some gimmicks have been allowed to creep in, despite the advice to the contrary. While a few regulars have asked about changing up the menu even more often and creating a weekly special, she recoils at the suggestion. "If it was weekly, I'd be unhappy! I'd put on a lot of weight from all the taste-testing," she says with a grin. "But I've always got volunteers here. When I'm trying to figure out the next special, our regulars are always happy to try it and give me their opinions. They are really happy." She stretches out that last word, miming a growing stomach.

Born in Drummondville, Héroux has that long connection to the Roy Jucep that her boss lacks. "I first came here when I was young, on outings with my dad. We ate poutine. Not with my mom or my family, just with my dad. I was lucky, because back then a dad and daughter outing wasn't that much of a thing," she says. Those kinds of memories—along with the good food—are what pull so many people back to the Jucep week after week.

Before it's time to leave the restaurant, I ask Lambert whether that nostalgia will be enough to keep the Roy Jucep going.

"Will it still be the same place in a decade, or will it change with the times? Or will it disappear when the next generation comes along?" I ask.

"I don't think it will disappear. This is the birthplace of a real national symbol, and it's not like we're isolated. We're only a five-minute drive off the Trans-Canada Highway," he says.

I interrupt him. "That's true, but very few Canadians have heard about it."

"No one is arguing for heritage status. The Roy Jucep's selling point is that it invented modern poutine," he tells us.

"But what's the value of that if no one outside Quebec knows the restaurant holds it?" I ask. "On menus around the world, poutine is described as a Quebec dish sometimes, a Canadian dish often or, more rarely, a Montreal dish."

"That's pretty much what I expect outside the country," Lambert responds. "People go to Montreal and they try the poutine there. They don't go to the regions to try it. They don't know to come here. So when people become convinced that poutine comes from Montreal, that's why."

Lambert pauses and reflects on his words. He's not completely satisfied with the entire situation as it stands. Despite the risk of enflaming local rivalries—and putting a stop to the debates that are so often settled by servers pointing to the certificate hanging on the restaurant's wall—Lambert wants the Quebec government to do something. It's time to "reappropriate poutine for the Centre-du-Québec" region, he says. As he speaks, his earlier resignation that poutine will just belong to Montreal because of the city's international exposure starts to fade, and he sounds hopeful for the future.

"We're brainstorming to see what we can do to take back our place as the inventor of poutine. People in Canada think it's Montreal. That makes no sense that people think it's Montreal. It makes no sense and we want to do something about it. We're not here to defend poutine against the rest of the planet—we don't have the money for that—but we can try for Canada," he concludes.

You could dismiss all this as a play for attention from the self-described numbers guy who wants a bigger share of the market. That might be a part of it, but as a local, he's also fully invested in furthering civic poutine pride. It's a win-win for him and Drummondville. The risks of a blowup with neighbours in the region are limited, he adds. Anyone else, any other restaurant with a real claim to poutine's history, has been closed for a very long time. The Jucep is the last link to that early history of Canada's dish.

The concerns of local rivalry and the fears of stepping on neighbouring toes seem to have faded since I spoke with Lambert. A local tourism agency in the Centre-du-Québec region has put out a poutine guide, complete with a map and a questionnaire directing you to the restaurants based on your flavour preferences. While some of the restaurants in the "Experience Poutine" guide are of questionable culinary quality, the region is finally turning toward its poutine history. The final question of the quiz drives home the whole point: "Where is poutine from?" the quirky test asks. You have two options: "Centre-du-Québec" or "Centre-du-Québec." You can't really go wrong.

Of course, Drummondville remains the heart of the region, and there's an ongoing push by locals to own a part of poutine's future. The heart of that effort isn't being spearheaded by any restaurant. Instead, for years, when no one else was willing to step forward and claim poutine, a rock band pretty much created the biggest thing in poutine from the back of a tour bus. In a province awash in festivals and poutine, the Festival de la Poutine de Drummondville still manages to stand out.

The band Les Trois Accords launched over a quarter century ago and has been a favourite of Quebec radio ever since. Born out of the 1990s punk and rock scene in Drummondville, the band's music is, in a word, big. The lyrics are fairly outrageous, filled with odd imagery and silly puns. Its records cover such offbeat topics as feelings for a friend's grandmother and how the province of Saskatchewan can steal someone's wife. While Les Trois Accords may have never made it big on the Prairies, the group was riding a high elsewhere in the mid-2000s. Their first album was selling well, and one of their hit songs, "Hawaïenne," had just been released as a single in France to wide acclaim. They even played as the opening act for the Rolling Stones—not the likeliest of pairings—for one of their tour stops in Canada.

With the band's fortunes rising and its members spending more time on the road, they started thinking more about their hometown. "We wanted to do something cultural for the city of Drummondville, to create the kind of festivals we'd seen in other cities," Simon Proulx, one of the band's cofounders, explains to me during a phone interview. "The idea for a poutine festival really came to us from Drummondville's real sense of paternity for poutine. There's a great pride in that."

Poutine was a constant in the band's touring of Quebec. Long hours, lots of time on the road and a ceaseless procession of chip trucks and *casse-croûtes* meant they often found themselves digging into one. Fans in towns across the province also had a habit of mobbing the band after shows and wanting to introduce them to the local variety of poutine. "It became a bit of a classic part of our tour to be told that a certain poutine in a certain part of Quebec was the best. We ended up testing a lot of poutines, and each of us had our own opinions about which was best. We argued a lot about that all the time. We started thinking it would really be great to have a festival that would celebrate that debate—and if it's a poutine festival, it really needs to be in Drummondville," Proulx says.

At the time, all five of the band's members were either from Drummondville or nearby villages. The idea of a poutine festival became a running gag for the band. During a moment of silence, one of them would always drop the idea of starting a festival for poutine. Laughter would follow. As Proulx explains, one of the reasons they never took the idea seriously is that they expected someone else would get around to doing it first. "It just couldn't be possible that there wouldn't be a poutine festival in Quebec. It would just be so strange for that not to exist," Proulx remembers thinking. Instead of doing something about it, the idea remained their favourite conversational crutch for years.

By 2005, the joke started to wear a little thin. The laughs slowly turned into serious contemplation, and the band began pulling together the paperwork they'd need for a festival. They went slow, expecting to hear that someone had scooped them and created a similar event first. The wheels ground forward with languid determination. They wrote up a budget, sent a letter to the municipal government and soon found themselves invited to city hall. It was a weird place for them to be, Proulx remembers. The band started reaching out to possible supporters and calling in favours from friends. One day they woke up and found themselves in the middle of organizing a poutine festival.

As we talk, years later and only a few weeks after the band has put out its latest album, the festival still looms large. Proulx is in the midst of an interview blitz about the album. I'd just heard him the other day on a major Montreal station, talking about their latest hit. Despite the intense pressure he was under, he said it wasn't much of a bother to squeeze in some time to talk about poutine. Sure, there's a lot of chaos in his life at the moment, but poutine is a relaxing kind of chaos for him. "I always have time for poutine," he says.

The band wasn't completely hopeless as it sketched out how to celebrate poutine. As a group, Les Trois Accords had helped put together concerts and had been acts at a number of music festivals. Luckily, they'd been preparing for years for this very moment. The band had done a lot of what Proulx describes as "spying" on other festivals. They kept notes on what seemed to work, what they enjoyed and what to avoid. They began putting together the festival by pulling out every scrap of paper and note with those ideas jotted on them.

What they quickly determined was that it wasn't really about poutine or music, but recapturing the heated arguments about the best poutines that would break out during quieter moments for the band. That was the fun part. It was the travel that fuelled those arguments, they realized—the exposure to new dishes and locals with strong opinions. So that's what they'd do: send out invites to poutine makers from across Quebec. Instead of going on tour, they'd bring all the poutine to them.

To convince people to travel to Drummondville, they'd throw in a performance, and they decided they just wanted to throw a music festival they'd want to attend with all their friends. "Putting that together, we convinced the city and our partners. That was easy. Where we had to put in most of the work at the start was the logistics at the festival. We learned a lot that first year on the ground. Lots of surprises. I think all festivals live through that," Proulx says.

As they were planning the first festival, set for the summer of 2008, poutine was undergoing rapid changes. Martin Picard at Montreal's Au Pied de Cochon was reconceptualizing poutine, pushing it into a new arena of international gastronomy. Picard's idea for poutine brought the dish somewhere it had never been before, shedding its rustic roots for ornate trappings. Along with crunchy fries, a dazzling squeak in the curds and a perfectly balanced gravy, his poutine would now feature a dab of foie gras.

In those last few years of the 2000s, poutine seemed to be taking off as a new national symbol. Even in Drummondville, they could feel it happening. Proulx describes the time as a crucial period when poutine went from being a Québécois icon to something decidedly more Canadian in the eyes of many outside the province. "We could feel that there was a wind behind poutine that was pushing it to be something bigger. I didn't expect what would happen. I certainly didn't expect that you could eventually get it almost everywhere in the world. That's pretty stunning. It's pretty cool."

The first festival, held only a kilometre from the Roy Jucep, began with a bang: over twenty thousand people showed up. Putting down a stake for poutine's hometown was a tremendous success. Unfortunately, the band hadn't really planned for how much of a success the festival would be—and they really hadn't been prepared for how popular the poutine itself would be. In retrospect, it seems like an obvious oversight, says Proulx. "We hadn't projected the enthusiasm for poutine. We knew people would want to eat poutine, but we really didn't have enough. Not at all enough poutine. People would line up for hours to get a poutine. We quickly realized that people were there for the poutine as much as the music, and we fixed that the next year."

While Proulx heard from locals worried that any kind of favouritism for Drummondville could upset the regional apple cart, he pushed aside the concerns. To this day, he says he shrugs off any debate that "isn't both passionate and also just for kicks." He agrees there's a cottage industry of debate in Quebec around poutine, from the best spot to the best ingredients. You could spend weeks on Facebook pages debating the minutiae of poutine. However, the lasting argument about where poutine originated is one that Proulx is willing to entertain: "Any debate on poutine's origin is mostly funny at this point. It's not contentious. There's something about it that adds to poutine's mystery," he says.

Quebecers and the province's poutine restaurants have taken to the festival's debate ethos. From gourmet kitchens to roadside eateries, the festival is open to anyone who can make a good poutine. The province's regional identities, from villages on the US border to northern towns, are on annual display. However, the one debate Proulx isn't too interested in is the ongoing question of whether poutine is Québécois or Canadian. He takes a factual and pretty literal approach to the argument. "That depends on whether you think Drummondville is in Canada," he says. "I think that's pretty straightforward. I think poutine should belong to the entire planet."

Despite the patchwork quilt of poutine from across Quebec, and the embracing of a diversity of regional styles and tastes, the festival is still clearly anchored in Drummondville. The message remains clear that this is poutine's home. There's no subtlety about that part of Les Trois Accords's plan. Even after more than fifteen years of festivals, they still want to ensure all Quebecers know the rich history.

"I don't know to what extent people across Quebec identify poutine as something coming from the Centre-du-Québec. When you grow up in Drummondville, you know that poutine is from here.

That's important. I think people should learn this in school. It should be a requirement," Proulx says, laughing.

"What would students in schools learn?" I ask. "Do they need to be told about Warwick's contribution as well?"

"It's usual with all great inventions that someone else wants to try to claim part of the paternity. Lots of inventions came from numerous places all at once. But students need to be told that there are certain things that needed to happen in the history of humanity. Like poutine."

I tell my dad later about the chat with Proulx, explaining that Les Trois Accords have been putting on a poutine and music festival. At first, he doesn't quite understand why. Then it clicks. "Oh, they are from Drummondville, those boys!" he says. But he doesn't know all that much about the band. I hum some of their songs; he's heard them on the radio, he's aware of them. "But it's not my style. I know them, but I don't know their songs all that much. I like to listen to the blues, old songs from Pink Floyd and Santana. That's my style. That's what I knew growing up. Les Trois Accords and Les Cowboys Fringants, that's the new style. I see them on TV sometimes. They seem nice." Needless to say, he won't be going to the poutine festival for the songs anytime soon.

Along with a cast of headliners that represents a solid who's who of Quebec's musical talent in any given year, the highlight of the festival is the annual awarding of the Golden Fork. It's the prize for the best poutine at each edition of the festival. There's an excitement growing in Proulx's voice as he talks about it. The Golden Fork began as a gag, at a festival that was itself once a bit of a gag among the band members. Despite its humble beginnings, however, the Golden Fork is now increasingly prized by restaurateurs. Every year, Proulx tells me, restaurants are pouring more and more effort into winning the thing.

"We were initially concerned that festivalgoers would be really prejudicial toward only voting for their own local poutines, but we've actually found that they really love trying new poutines and voting for restaurants that aren't from around here. That makes it a better victory when Drummondville wins because you know people are being as impartial as they can be," Proulx continues. The prize is decided based on a popular vote of all festivalgoers, and fun is at the core of it all. As he explains it, the entire competition is a hands-on-hearts kind of business; there's no independent jury and no accounting firm to supervise the results. While it's all pretty rudimentary, the crowd's popular choice generally reflects a pretty darn good poutine.

Martin Picard, that innovator of gastronomic poutine, has attended a number of the poutine festivals as a guest, to pass on knowledge and spread the good word, but he's never actually entered the award competition. His brand of food likely wouldn't be a great fit for the high-volume crowd or the music-festival vibe of the affair, says Proulx. "Martin Picard has helped so much over the last fifteen years by creating the vision that poutine isn't just junk food. I think there's a growing sense that poutine can be very well made, that it can be a food that's valuable and of high quality when it's made right," he adds. With that, Proulx needs to wrap up our call—he's got another interview about his new album.

The all-time champion of the Golden Fork, with three wins so far, is the Cantine Chez Ben. It's a long-standing fry joint that specializes in poutine and hot dogs in Granby, a small city about an hour south of Montreal.

A few months after talking with Proulx, I make my way to Granby to try the championship poutine. I'd turned on the navigation to find my way to the casual joint but I needn't have bothered. Standing in front of the restaurant is a ten-metre neon sign that is strikingly unmistakable. In a constellation of bright lights, the sign is an enormous representation of Ben La Bedaine, the restaurant's mascot, eating a hot dog with one hand and holding a platter with a burger and fries in the other. "Chez Ben" is written in bright red lights on the front of his apron, and the words "*On s'bour la bédaine*" continue down toward the neon chef's knees: at Ben's, we stuff our tummy. It's as much a prediction as it is an order.

While there's more rural Quebec nostalgia here, much like what I'd seen at the Roy Jucep, Ben's sign is a little beaten up at this point. There's been an attempt in recent years to bring some effervescence back to the peeling, weathered emblem, according to its owners, but the effort has been stymied by the sign's age. There aren't many people left who know how to fix neon this old. To help preserve the sign for future generations, the town is also planning to give it local heritage status, something befitting one of Granby's true attractions. That says a lot in a town that also hosts one of Canada's busiest zoos.

Just past the enormous sign is the Golden Fork–winning poutine. I arrive late in the afternoon and there's a line the length of the restaurant, but it moves fast. The staff are in the same shirts as Ben wears on the giant sign, with thick red and white stripes. They even wear red chef's wedge hats. If it wasn't for the flat-screen TVs displaying the menus, you could imagine yourself being in the 1960s. The rest of the place is utilitarian, with plastic trays, plastic chairs and plastic tables. Despite the impressively varied menu, most orders are for poutine. This is, as another sign outside boasts, "*la meilleure poutine.*"

A few minutes after I order a regular poutine, my number is called. It's delivered in an aluminum bowl, and in the few steps it takes to get it to my table, I'm already getting anxious to dig in. The gravy is dark and thick, its fragrance heading straight to my brain stem. Before I can think more about it, I see the thick-cut fries the restaurant uses. They're freshly cut and crispy. Finally, the cheese curds. They are once again perfect. The large, glistening chunks absolutely dominate the bowl.

Sitting down, I grasp my fork and take my first bite. The ingredients are in perfect balance: thick gravy on thick fries with thick curds. It's simple but packs a flavourful punch in every bite. This is how poutine should taste. I can understand why the restaurant's mantel is getting heavy with awards.

As I drive back to Montreal afterwards, I think about how poutine seems to be slowly drifting away from Ben's simplicity. While my road trip with my dad is focused on poutine's history, and classic diners like the Roy Jucep and the Princesse, that's not the way poutine is going. In the suburbs outside the city, as the traffic starts building up, I spot a bright Fromagerie Victoria sign off the highway. Behind it is the latest in a fast-growing franchise focused on poutine, with a menu that goes beyond the traditional. A shift toward more exotic offerings is underway across the province.

Over the past fifteen years, Drummondville's festival has given Quebecers a distinct perch from which to view the ongoing changes to poutine. Along with becoming more common throughout Quebec, Canada and the world, the dish has shed some of its earlier baggage. The stigma that it's a working-class, rural and francophone dish has largely faded away. Instead, year after year, the offerings at the festival have been both wilder and from farther away. While some chefs have gone looking for exotic ingredients, the culinary leaps have not always been appreciated by the gathered aficionados. The audiences know poutine well and don't appreciate expensive ingredients covering a poor base. So much of what works best and wins awards is still creating that perfect mixture of fries, gravy and cheese curds.

The Roy Jucep won its first Golden Fork in 2022. Despite earlier worries that locals would only cast a ballot for local establishments, voters had looked at other options for over a decade. Coming out of a pandemic that disrupted the world, the Roy Jucep's fries and cheese served as a large comfort blanket for attendees seeking a return to normalcy. At least that's the best theory as to why the restaurant won. There was ample cheering and pride when the result was announced, and the Golden Fork headed to a home it had never known before.

The win for the Roy Jucep made me reflect back to my time speaking with Charles Lambert. While nearly everyone else at the restaurant had spoken about their poutine with a glint in their eyes, telling me how it's part of their personal story, describing the ingredients in such emotional detail, Lambert never did. He had been very matter-of-fact about that specific component of his business—the whole eating and enjoying it part. I figured that was partly because he's a hard-nosed businessman. While we were speaking, he was constantly scanning the restaurant and passing on a thought or observation to the manager or the nearest member of the waitstaff. Lambert was also clearly more comfortable with big plans, exacting details and specific facts than squishy topics like poutine's cultural impact. But he hadn't really spoken about the dish itself.

I thought about how that conversation had ended. As my dad and I got up to leave the Roy Jucep, I asked Lambert, "Do you like poutine?"

"I'm actually not a big fan of poutine. I might eat it twice a year here. Not too often because I want to keep in shape. But we don't need to talk about that," he said with a wave. "There's nothing bad in the poutine. And I've had lots of opportunities to eat it. I've seen it everywhere. I saw it at Disney on Main Street. I've had it in Costa Rica and in Paris. I go to Montana every year and they've got it at a bar in Billings. It was a new thing for them. They had a sign that said, 'We now serve poutine.' I told the waitress that I know poutine, that I own the restaurant that invented it."

"Did she believe you?" I asked.

"I don't know."

"Did you order it?"

"No."

CHAPTER FIVE

The poutine highway

B Y EXPLORING THE BIRTH OF POUTINE, MY FATHER AND I WERE beginning to learn something about the nature of invention itself. Even the most revolutionary changes usually come through an evolutionary process. While invention in the public's imagination is often confined to the image of a genius working away in a basement or garage, that's rarely the case. Thomas Edison did not come up with the light bulb alone. While his name appears on a US patent numbered 223,898, the light bulb came out of a New Jersey laboratory that was fully staffed with engineers and tinkerers. Edison said he was sitting alone and absentmindedly fiddling with a piece of carbon when it came to him. But after that eureka moment for the filament that would light the world, he still needed a team of scientists to come up with a working light bulb.

Poutine didn't come out of a vacuum either. Its laboratory is an area of small-town Quebec stretching from Drummondville up an otherwise unassuming rural highway that ends across the St. Lawrence River from Quebec City. And from the original mothers and fathers of poutine, an entire cast of characters is responsible for getting the dish to where it is now. Some of them have appeared in the pages of the world's greatest magazines and newspapers over the past two decades, while others in the story have worked in total anonymity. Jean-Paul Roy, Fernand Lachance and Eddy Lainesse get much of the credit for poutine's invention, but there were many more hands in that kitchen.

To become the dish we know today, poutine needed to find a way out of its cradle in rural Quebec. Not just from one small town to the next, but to a critical mass of Quebecers. To make that move, the dish hitched a ride in the stomach of a twenty-three-year-old from Quebec City named Ashton Leblond.

Once again, many months later, I find myself in my dad's car. With two cups of steaming coffee and a winter storm covering the province under a foot of snow, we head north to the end of the poutine highway.

"What's the name of this place?" my dad asks.

"It's Chez Ashton. It's really well-known in Quebec City," I tell him.

"I know the name of the restaurant," he says with uncertainty in his voice. "But I've never been there. Are they only in Quebec City?"

"Yes," I reply. The traffic is light, and to either side of the highway, the dense forest looks like a postcard of a winter wonderland. "In and around the city."

"I really couldn't tell you if it's good or bad poutine," my dad says. "I've been to Quebec City a few times for work. I was there in the 1980s while building pipelines. I ate a lot of poutine and chicken when I was there. Maybe I went there, I don't know."

"Well, we're going to find out. It was certainly there in the 1980s," I tell him.

When it comes to poutine in Quebec's capital today, Leblond's name stands above all others. He's unquestionably one of the big figures in poutine's history. Back in 1969, he opened a small *casse-croûte* in the suburbs and his venture grew from there. It went through a few names early on but soon would be known by the one that would stick: Chez Ashton. From that one location, the chain would grow to twenty-five restaurants.

He's speaking with me over the phone from his home in Florida, where he's avoiding the harsh Canadian winter. I've called him to learn how poutine's presence expanded in Quebec City.

Leblond's first poutine was a fortuitous moment that he still remembers today. He was young and eager to learn what he could. His restaurant was getting by, but it wasn't a hit yet. He travelled to Victoriaville in 1972 to visit his brother, who owned a small restaurant outside of that town. He'd told Ashton that he was going to add poutine to his menu.

Speaking to me a half century later, Leblond remembers being intrigued. "I'd never heard of a poutine before," he says. So the two set off to the local *fromagerie* to try it out, and somehow they got their hands on curds, gravy and fries. Leblond had been in the restaurant business for two years. He was a novice. But after popping those first few bites of poutine into his mouth, he says he immediately knew he was holding a winner in his hands. Then and there, he decided he would bring poutine to Quebec City.

Like all the early characters that created poutine or helped it along in its early days, Leblond's youth was thoroughly coloured by rural Quebec. He was born in 1948 in a small village with the wonderfully long name of Saint-François-Xavier-de-Brompton. Near Sherbrooke in Quebec's Eastern Townships, the village was far from poutine's heartland and the cultural turbulence underway elsewhere in the province. Instead, Leblond's youth mirrored that of many young Quebecers of the era. He was raised on a struggling family farm with eighteen brothers and sisters, who were all expected to contribute to the hard work that began before dawn and continued until well past dusk every day.

It was twelve years after Fernand Lachance mixed fries and cheese together in Warwick for the first time, and more broadly, Quebec was in turmoil. The province was in the midst of its Quiet Revolution. A fragile stasis from decades of deeply conservative government was suddenly replaced by a confusing technicolour of politics. Modernity came knocking in a hurry. A new generation of politicians was now in the halls of Quebec's legislature, the National Assembly. They had an ambitious agenda to build a new society, with French-Canadian leaders at the centre of it.

Along with the wholesale change of the world around them, this group was also grappling with the newly pressing question of whether Quebec should remain within Canada. Only three years after joining the federal Liberal Party, Pierre Trudeau entered the Prime Minister's Office in 1968 at the helm of the federal government. He was a modernizer who was stridently pro-Canada. In Quebec, René Lévesque had gone from being a star provincial Liberal candidate in 1960 to becoming a pivotal part of the French-Canadian renaissance in government. He increasingly found himself on the other side of the debate over Quebec's future. By 1968, he left the Liberals and was at the forefront of a burgeoning movement to make Quebec its own state. The two men were friends and intellectual adversaries who debated often in public on Radio-Canada and in private at the dinner table as their respective political convictions grew increasingly at odds. A crowd of Quebec separatists rioted that same year, throwing rocks and bottles at Trudeau during a Saint-Jean-Baptiste Day parade in Montreal. The newly minted prime minister stood his ground and stared down the rioters. Fractures over the national question began appearing in homes and businesses across Quebec. Some of those remain to this day.

In the midst of that chaos and political violence, Leblond saw the limitations of his family farm and, still only a teenager, left to make a name for himself. He quickly ended up in Quebec City. After working in kitchens and picking up bits of the cooking trade here and there, he began working at a college near the capital's airport when he was seventeen. He credits those years as his "cooking university," where he learned his way around a kitchen and, more importantly, how to make gravy. He saved up as much money as he could. His dream was to wait until he was twenty-one and then strike out on his own. As his twenty-first year approached, he found a chip wagon for sale near Sherbrooke. He planned to drag it to Quebec City and hang an "open" sign during the warm months. "I convinced my dad to lend me $5,000. That was serious money. There was just no margin of error," he says.

Leblond promised his dad he'd repay the loan as quickly as he could. He had crunched the numbers and was sure he could make it work, though it might take a while. The small restaurant opened in 1969, selling a bottle of Coca-Cola for five cents. The twenty-one-year-old Leblond took on some workers, paying the then minimum wage of $1 an hour. "That $5,000 really was a lot of money," he repeats. Chez Ashton was born.

The fry shack was more of a large recreational vehicle than a trailer, with "Ashton Snack-Bar" written across the top. The better-known name would come soon enough. The wheels quickly came off, on purpose and literally, as it became a permanent fixture in the increasingly busy capital. Lambert set up shop at a busy crossroads in L'Ancienne-Lorette, a suburban enclave surrounded by Quebec City. Unlike some of the earlier diners near Drummondville that had added poutine to their menus, this wasn't rural Quebec. The competition was ferocious from the first day, with many locals already having a favourite greasy spoon for lunch or supper. Leblond had to convince them to steer his way and try something new. "I first tried advertising meatloaf along with hot dogs," he says. For hot dogs, he had both grilled and the steamed variety popular in Quebec. He also offered hamburgers and fries, as well as a fries and gravy combo, but that wasn't a great seller.

In 1972, after trying poutine in Victoriaville, he added it to the menu of his snack bar. As far as I've been able to find, this was the first time poutine appeared at a restaurant outside of its home region of Centre-du-Québec. That lack of previous geographic spread soon became apparent as Leblond immediately ran into a significant problem. Quebec City had no *fromageries* making cheese curds. He had to pay someone to drive down to Victoriaville to pick up curds for each day's poutines, a nearly three-hour round trip.

"We just put it up on the menu. We didn't know whether anyone would enjoy it. There was no celebration, no balloons. I was personally sold on it, but the first time I brought it to the fry shack, all my employees from the Quebec City area were hesitant. None wanted to try it." What followed was an eight-year slog where nearly every day, he had to explain what poutine was. From pronunciation to the basic ingredients, Leblond had to sell it one client at a time. "People in Quebec City didn't eat any cheese curds. I really had to push hard. I had to work just to get people to try it," he remembers.

I wish I could write that poutine helped fuel Quebec's Quiet Revolution, but it didn't. Similar forces of modernity were propelling both the province's social upheaval and the emergence of quick dining. But the comparisons end quite abruptly. The history only helps paint the context of the era in which poutine evolved.

One explanation for poutine's early snubbing in Quebec City is that the dish appeared at the start of what would be decades of enormous social stigma among Quebecers. There were few problems of that kind when poutine remained in the small villages and towns of rural Quebec. However, as Daniel Béland, director of the McGill Institute for the Study of Canada, explained to me, once poutine made it to the cities, it was seen as painfully rural by some. Instead of being a treat, cheese curds were seen as parochial and demonstrative of a lack of interest in finer foods. Once that hurdle was cleared and people realized that poutine was pretty darn delicious, the stigma shifted to one of class.

Many in the province's increasingly powerful intelligentsia wouldn't want to be seen anywhere near a poutine. "Poutine was seen as painfully proletarian," according to Béland. It's simply unthinkable that the intellectual giants of the era, like Pierre Trudeau or René Lévesque, would ever be caught eating a poutine. The patrician Trudeau would likely scoff at the dish, unfortunately, while the Montrealer Lévesque actually had a taste for simpler rural cuisine like pea soup, but that was mostly as an expression of tradition. Poutine was both new and somewhat suspect. The same feelings would hold true for the new class of bureaucrats and other business leaders converging in Quebec City. Poutine just wasn't on the menu for them yet.

Leblond wasn't going to give up easily on convincing Quebec City that poutine should be on their plates. To win over hesitant diners, he started handing out free samples. He had a captive audience. People waiting for their lunch orders at picnic tables by the *casse-croûte* would get small cups of poutine. There would be three or four cheese curds, a few fries, hot gravy and a toothpick. He did that every day for years. He kept faith in poutine, when all indicators pointed to it being a flop in the making that could take his restaurant down with it. Most of his staff was telling him to drop it. But what started as a need to set himself apart from competitors quickly turned into a mission to educate an entire city of reluctant diners. "I knew it could take off. That's why I stuck with it," he says. "I knew it."

There was a lot for the young chef to like. Poutine is a quintessentially modern food, it's quick to make and its ingredients are relatively inexpensive, minus some gas money. The poutine that Leblond inherited was also starting to evolve, picking up new types of diners with a growing variety of new tastes as it moved along the poutine highway. The three original ingredients would remain a permanent fixture but, by the early 1970s, they were joined by a growing cast of supporting characters. For the first time, chefs began tossing in chicken, green peas, spaghetti sauce and hot dogs to bulk up poutine—though not usually together. These first variations have since become old favourites.

After almost five years, tens of thousands of samples and hundreds of thousands of explanations of what a poutine was, people finally started showing up to order it. After a lot of spilled gravy, Leblond finally had a star on his menu. For poutine, this marks the moment when the rural descriptor could be dropped. It now belonged to all of Quebec.

Outside Leblond's fry wagon, Quebec City was still a sleepy capital. Despite significant growth in the province's civil service as a more assertive state built up its French-speaking bureaucracy, the city's cramped central neighbourhoods saw little population growth. As he handed out free samples, the area around Leblond seemed stuck in stasis as political leaders dreamt up entirely new health and education systems from scratch to replace the Catholic Church. Just beyond Chez Ashton, Quebec City's suburbs were spreading out alongside new highways, with builders throwing up kilometres of bungalows. The new developments, with their cul-de-sacs, were aided by a new suspension bridge being strung across the St. Lawrence River. Over a kilometre in length, the new bridge would be named after Pierre Laporte.

Laporte's name is now synonymous with the political violence of the era. He was Quebec's deputy premier in 1970 when he was kidnapped and then murdered by members of the Front de Libération du Quebec, a small group of terrorists who wanted Quebec independence at any cost. As part of its vague plan to turn Quebec into a Marxist paradise, the FLQ had earlier engaged in a bombing campaign before kidnapping a British diplomat. Unlike Laporte, diplomat James Cross was released unharmed but shaken by the FLQ after two months of captivity. He would die a lifetime later in England during the COVID-19 pandemic. However, the October Crisis that followed Laporte's abduction saw prime minister Pierre Trudeau invoke the country's War Measures Act, unleashing police raids that arrested 497 people and sending soldiers onto the province's streets. It was an unprecedented moment in Canada's peacetime history and a sign of a fraying debate in the province, with some armchair revolutionaries cheering on political violence from the sidelines. Why stop at the creation of business giants and an assertive new state when you could become your own country? After the widespread arrests of October, the moderate and separatist Parti Québécois would form government for the first time in 1976.

Instead of Quebec City, most of the province's middle class gravitated toward Montreal. That city was still Canada's economic and cultural capital, sitting at the apex of its prestige in a confident country that was entering its second century. Expo 67 had ended as one of the most successful and memorable world's fairs of the twentieth century, with millions walking through the turnstiles. Its success had made the city a global player. Now, the metropolis was preparing to repeat the performance with the 1976 Summer Olympics. Lightning did not strike twice. Those games would be marked by disastrous cost overruns and, amid outstanding athletics, a boycott by twenty-nine African countries. It seemed like another perfect exemplar of the glamorous 1960s giving way to a far darker 1970s.

For Leblond, things were finally looking up by 1976. He outgrew his trailer as business boomed and built his first permanent restaurant. This was the start of the Chez Ashton that would become a local icon. Diners were starting to like poutine, but Leblond wasn't quite done tinkering with the dish. Much like the founder of the Roy Jucep, he wanted to work on perfecting his gravy recipe. What he'd used so far was based on the gravy used for a hot chicken sandwich—another popular dish in Quebec diners that consisted of shredded chicken and green peas in a bread roll, with the entire thing covered in a generous pour of hot gravy.

Speaking decades later, Leblond is pretty mum about what came next with his sauce. He doesn't want to reveal any secrets, but he's proud of what he made. He worked on the gravy for years, making it browner and more flavourful. The original had been a little too sweet for his taste. "That improved gravy was part of the reason for my success," he tells me. "A good poutine needs a truly excellent sauce to pull the entire dish together."

Those free samples were now paying off big time. Poutine was on a roll in Quebec City, fuelling Chez Ashton. The wheel of expansion started turning, and Leblond opened a second restaurant in 1981, just as he entered his mid-thirties. Poutine kept growing.

"When I started, I never thought poutine would become this popular. I thought it would eventually do well, but not like this. Poutine today is Quebec's most typical meal. It has really become something identified with our province. It identifies us," he says.

Back in my dad's car, the snow outside is falling steadily. We'd thought about calling off our trip to Chez Ashton, but my dad wanted to press on. "I didn't expect this much of a *tempête*," he says, allowing himself to relax for the first time in a half-hour after keeping an intense focus on the slippery highway.

I nod. "I'll drive on the way back, but we're going to need to change the music," I say. We've had one of his Pink Floyd discs on repeat.

"Ashton is seen like the father of poutine around here," I tell my dad. In the distance now we see the Pierre Laporte Bridge and Quebec City beyond it.

"I hope it's good. He's going to have a lot of competition," my dad says.

While most people know Quebec's capital from postcard photos of the old town and the Château Frontenac, we're driving on a modern highway with subdivisions stretching into the distance. I'd been living in Edmonton after a job transfer, and driving through suburban Quebec City, I could imagine I was back in Alberta's capital.

Our destination today isn't the quaint Basse-Ville neighbourhood of Quebec City, with its narrow alleys and historic flair. Instead, we're out in the city's outskirts where that first Chez Ashton was built. The restaurant is still standing and quite busy, so we need to go hunting in the back for a parking spot. "This looks like a nice place," my dad tells me.

As he and I come around to the front, we see that the line is nearly out the door. We join it. There's nothing letting patrons know that this location is the oldest in the chain, other than the fact that many locals have been driving past for decades. The decor inside is simple, with red benches and unadorned tables. The menu isn't much more complicated, with burgers, hot dogs and poutines.

Despite its length, the line moves so quickly that I find myself in front of the cash register before I've decided what I want. The staff, wearing old-fashioned black wedge caps, give me a hard look as I look up at the menu. In a rush, we order two steamed hot dogs and a regular poutine, along with a small poutine augmented with sausages. It's the most popular add-on at the moment. "Don't go anywhere," the floor manager tells me as I move down the counter after paying. "Two poutines. It'll be here in a minute."

Chez Ashton has some of the fastest service I've ever seen. Five minutes after I put in our order, we're sitting at one of the nearby tables with our food. The poutines look great. The fries are crispy and golden. The cheese is squeaky and fresh—not quite as mind-blowing as what we had in Princeville but great for a chain's offering. My dad says little as he eats—nothing will make you hungrier than a long drive spent clenching the steering wheel. The gravy is a little darker and saltier than what we've had elsewhere, but it's a welcome change. Chez Ashton is fast, delicious and relatively cheap. "It's not bad at all," my dad tells me. "I think the snow is moving north, but we should get out of here before the storm worsens."

I take a moment before we leave to look around the restaurant and reflect on my notes from my call with Leblond. While he's widely recognized in the capital for bringing poutine to Quebec's second-largest city, he didn't invent it. But for many of his patrons, he perfected it.

"Most people in Quebec ate their first poutine at our place, and they've stayed loyal to our poutine. I really like that. They taste it somewhere else and then they come home to us," he told me over the phone.

Leblond is also known for embracing the idea that some variations of poutine should be encouraged. While a far cry from the relative upstarts that serve a nearly unfathomable number of permutations of poutine, Chez Ashton's modern menu has evolved into three dishes. Each is a hit in its own right.

The top of the menu is reserved for Leblond's prize: the authentic Ashton poutine. It has fries made from local potatoes, the squeakiest curds he can find and his secret homemade brown gravy.

His second variety is the Dulton, Leblond's favourite. It has the authentic poutine as its base but is topped with spiced ground beef. The beef and cheese curds give the poutine a taste profile that'll chase rings around your tongue.

Finally, the *galvaude* makes an appearance on Chez Ashton's menu as well. Breaking the convention of many of his competitors, Leblond doesn't call it a poutine. It's a mix to him, as the dish forgoes cheese curds for chunks of white chicken meat and green peas. He argues that a proper poutine needs the three original ingredients, even if you plan on adding more to it.

There are also lots of pop-up specials, like the poutine we're eating that is mixed with pieces of sausage. My dad doesn't even try it. "I'll stick with the original," he tells me. I take a few bites. I'll finish it, but I also could stick with the original.

"This isn't the first time I've been to Ashton. But it was very different my first time," I say to my dad. He gestures for me to tell him more.

Like many Quebecers who have been to Leblond's restaurant, my first poutine at Chez Ashton was just after 2 a.m. following a merry night of drinking during my university days. The restaurant in the middle of Quebec City's downtown was a madhouse, with long lines snaking wildly as barely coherent students were drawn toward the smell of fries and gravy. I have never regretted a post-midnight poutine and that night was no different. However, the long history linking a fortifying poutine with the end of the evening might now be drawing to a close.

For decades, Chez Ashton was synonymous with the late-night popularity of poutine, open until 4 a.m. and home to a crowd. "But today, that barely exists anymore," Leblond told me. While it might sound like a complaint about the next generation, he had the sales data. "Young people just aren't up as late, and it isn't the same anymore. I've only got one location, the one in downtown Quebec City, that's still open around the clock, but that's it." That's the restaurant I'd visited that first time.

"There's one more thing Leblond told me that's interesting," I tell my dad. "On a cold day like this in January, our poutine would be cheaper.

"For three weeks in early January, the restaurant gives people a discount based on the temperature the previous night. If it was minus thirty degrees Celsius, the poutine is thirty per cent off the next day. He tells me there's a lineup so long for the cheaper poutine that people end up standing outside in the cold."

My dad laughs. "*Ah ben, j'ai mon voyage.* I've never heard of anything like that!"

We get back into my dad's car. It takes me a minute to adjust the seat and mirrors—he's nearly a foot shorter than me. As we join the traffic out of Quebec City, I remember the end of my conversation with Leblond.

"Poutine isn't losing its popularity for now. It's like pizza to me. I hope it's going to continue through the years. What's important is knowing how to make it and giving it all the flavour it deserves," said Leblond, his voice relaxing. "I really get disappointed when people tell me that poutine is too fatty, that the sauce is too dark or that there's something else about poutine they don't like. You need to know how to appreciate it. There is good pizza and not so good. Poutine is the same way."

Seen in the rear-view mirror, poutine's ascendency can look like a straight line from rural obscurity to the world stage. But it wasn't such a sure thing. Leblond can't claim the title of inventor, but his efforts to ensure poutine became Quebec's national dish suggest he should be recognized as a poutine patron.

Even as he was breathing in the air of the Everglades, Leblond told me he can't ever truly get away from poutine. When travelling Quebecers learn who he is, they always want to chat with Mr. Chez Ashton. "They always tell me they are looking forward to getting a poutine once they get back to Quebec. That's home."

CHAPTER SIX

Three ingredients in Trois-Rivières

I FIRST SET OUT WITH MY FATHER TO DISCOVER WHERE POUTINE had been created. But back in Trois-Rivières, it's the people we met and the stories they told us that I'm left thinking about: Virginie Gadbois working a poutine counter in Warwick as a way of remembering her dad; Charles Lambert prepping gravy in his garage to protect the recipe for his secret sauce; and the twinkle in Yolande Morissette's eyes as she remembers poutine's early days. The big story we're trying to find is suddenly much clearer.

Along with cheese curds and a burning necessity to improvise, poutine's history was punctuated by more stubbornness and vision than I'd expected. With poutine now burrowing into Quebec City through the efforts of Chez Ashton, it's time to head back to the Centre-du-Québec. It's time to finish what we started.

Our trusty Ford is filled up with gas and we are going to continue our journey in my dad's hometown of Saint-Léonard-d'Aston. The Lamothe family lived on the outskirts of the village for generations, tilling the land and tapping maple trees. Saint-Léonard-d'Aston is a small farming village, with just over two thousand people mostly clustered around a Catholic church, a Desjardins credit union and a few *casse-croûtes* now doing a brisk trade in poutine. Up until recently, the village was best known as the home of Le Madrid, which long competed for the prize of most eccentric restaurant in Quebec. A pit stop alongside the Trans-Canada Highway, Le Madrid pulled in passing motorists with outstanding kitsch and an impressive plastic menagerie on its grounds that seemed to always be growing following its opening in 1967. As a child, I kept my nose pressed up against the car window to look at the monster trucks and massive fibreglass dinosaurs that loomed over the highway as we drove past. It was worth the look. There were eventually seventy-five dinosaurs in the huge parking lot outside the restaurant, which was built with an inexplicably Spanish-inspired architecture that gave it its name. The fake dinosaurs were frozen in scenes chasing and frolicking with each other, protecting Le Madrid's whitewashed castle turret and its big neon sign promising buffet dining and workers who speak English. It was a landmark, big in every way.

As we drove past this time on Highway 20, the Le Madrid I knew was missing. I quickly learned that it was a victim of its own success. The owners had sold the restaurant and its eclectic collection to a property developer, who brought in a wrecking ball. The kitsch was mostly auctioned off, with a few of the smaller dinosaurs put to work in a new kids' play area. The roadside stop was rebuilt around a generic building that hosted a McDonald's and was christened Le Madrid 2.0. Instead of a large billboard outside advertising the inexpensive and locally sourced poutine that had built up a cult following over decades, the main publicity as we drove past this time was for the McCafé. Fully caffeinated for the morning, we did not stop.

"You want to go to the *fromagerie*?" my dad asks.

"Absolutely!" I blurt out. My mind quickly forgets the missing dinosaurs. This is the *fromagerie* where my father had worked all those years earlier, the place where his story comes closest to lining up with those formative years of poutine. There's silence as he drives the streets of the village, takes a right turn and puts his car into park. We're sitting outside a squat yellow brick building on the edge of the village's main drag. The structure has that institutional feel of so many buildings thrown up after World War I—all simple lines and faded brick. It's also in a state of disrepair, with broken windows and plywood boards covering some doors.

"This was the Produits Laitiers Aston. This is where all the milk came and the cheese curds were made," he finally tells me, breaking the silence. There's real admiration in his voice as he goes over the lines of the building with his eyes. Despite the state of the place, my dad is clearly starting to fizz with excitement.

The *fromagerie* changed hands a number of times after my dad left in the late 1960s. Back then it was just one of the small cheese factories that dotted Quebec, owned by a local bigwig who was also Saint-Léonard-d'Aston's mayor. It was eventually sold to Lactantia, before the diary giant shut it down as part of a wave of consolidation. I spot a sign that explains the building has taken on a new life as an oversized storage shed for lumber owned by the BMR hardware store across the street.

My dad unclips his seat belt. "Alright, let's go in," he says, getting out of the car.

"We can't just walk right into the building," I tell him. He shrugs. "Let me go find someone to explain what we're doing," I say.

I head into the yard in front of the hardware store and find a manager—he's clearly harried and his radio keeps going off—and tell him I'd like to walk around with my dad in the building across the street.

"It's a shed," he tells me, obviously wondering what's actually going on.

"My dad used to work in there when it was a *fromagerie* and he wants to take a look around," I tell him.

He waves us on with a shrug. "Go ahead."

We enter through a side door and my dad's eyes go wide as he walks into the main space of the building. "This is where it happened," he says. His arms come alive and he starts pointing at where things once were. "That's where we had the basins where I made the cheese," he adds quickly. "The equipment is gone, but I can see where it all was. See those rings on the floor? That's where the separators once were." He hasn't been here in decades, not since he was a young man. Much has changed, but there are still quite a few signs of what once was.

The long room is now packed with lumber, but the ghosts of a past life start swirling as he speaks. That small mark on the wall? "That's where a critical piece of equipment once was anchored," he says. That oddity over in the corner where there's a deep dip in the floor? "That's where cheese curds were packaged," he continues. "I worked with a lot of good guys in this room, hardworking guys." The main doors to the production room, where cheese was made for generations, are long gone. The hole is now filled in by cheap cinder blocks.

That excited energy from our first poutine chat, years ago, has returned. I've rarely seen him so animated, just gliding across the floor and talking like a professional tour guide after downing an espresso. You'd never know from the perceptible bounce in his step that he's waiting for a knee replacement.

A few hardware store workers are looking on in amusement until they realize we're talking about poutine.

"This place has something to do with the history of poutine?" one of them asks.

My dad doesn't miss a beat. "This used to be a *fromagerie*. Right here, this building. And we were churning out cheese curds when those first ever poutines were being made," he explains. They nod. Together, the workers begin looking around the worn building with newfound admiration.

That's when the store's manager, who I spoke with earlier, comes in to see what the fuss is all about. He likely realized that letting two people who came in off the street with a paper-thin alibi walk through a building stuffed with expensive lumber and renovation supplies wasn't his best call of the day.

Before he can say anything, my dad is moving on. "This is the way through to the laboratory where we used to test the cheese curds," he tells me. The manager relaxes a bit and joins the group, quickly realizing that the short old man, my dad, really does seem to know what he's talking about. Despite its rotten state on the outside, the core of the old building still holds traces of its history.

"This was the main production room. It's a really well-built space," my dad tells us. The manager draws our attention to the series of massive wooden beams that span the ceiling of the vast room. They'd been cut locally from ancient forests nearly a century ago. While the beams have a humble job now, covering plywood and lumber, the store's manager says that an insurance adjustor recently estimated the value of the thirteen wooden beams at $195,000. That was considered "a conservative estimate." If BMR ever wanted to build a new storage shed, each of those beams would be taken down and sold.

"What would someone do with them?" I ask, surprised.

"They'd likely become the polished bar for a trendy restaurant in Montreal or Toronto. You could do something beautiful with that wood," he says. The hardware manager makes it clear he'd expect to fetch top dollar for those beams.

My dad had been nodding along, but he's already moved on. Like a sudden hurricane, he takes me, the two workers and the manager deeper into the building. I'm too caught up in this, whatever this is, to feel the pride bubbling up.

The old milk laboratory is now unused and filled with rubbish. It looks like a school laboratory in some post-apocalyptic movie—miraculously, there are still beakers and delicate scales sitting on the dark wooden counter, all covered in dust. I peek into a formica cabinet and there's more laboratory equipment that appears decades old.

"This is where farm milk would be tested, just to make sure it hadn't gone off somewhere between the cows and *fromagerie*," my dad explains. I'm amazed that so much of the original, Korean War–vintage equipment is still around.

"We don't really come in here," says the manager. There's no time to wait around. My father bounds up a flight of old wooden stairs and ends up in an area with furnishings straight out of the 1950s. This blue-collar set from the era before *Mad Men* is where milk workers once changed. It's now stuffed with rolled pink insulation mats, thrown over mid-century modern chairs and tables. "We use this place," says the manager. His radio goes off and he excuses himself.

This is the industrial side of poutine's past. It isn't automation and antiseptic stainless steel but hardwood floors and vinyl armchairs. Despite some of the softer edges that you can still see decades later, this *fromagerie* was highly productive back in its heyday. "They made much more cheese than anyone could eat around here," my dad says. The cheese went off to Montreal and even England—but more importantly, the cheese curds ended up in gas stations and restaurants across central Quebec.

"This was a good place to work," my dad says with a sigh. He tells the hardware store workers more stories as we head out, leaving them and me with a sense that history can still live unappreciated around us. He stands in the main room again, one last time, and stares for a long while before turning around and leaving.

He'll call me early the next morning and tell me he wants to talk about his dreams that night. I can't emphasize enough how much my dad is not the kind of man who has ever used those words before. I rush over to his place. He'd spent his sleeping hours back in the cheese factory, walking the floors with coworkers he hadn't thought about in a half century. "I could see that factory like it once was. They were all there, we were talking. It was incredible," he tells me. The smells and weight of the cheese curds and milk jugs had come tumbling back into his consciousness.

He said it was one of the most vivid, incredible experiences he'd ever had. We'd walked around what is now a hardware store storage shed, but he'd gone somewhere else in his mind and brought us on the trip with him. He'd spend the next few years thinking about our visit and those dreams.

After leaving the old *fromagerie*, we decide to walk to the one-room town hall to see if they have anything on file about the business's history. There's a *casse-croûte* advertising poutine next door to the building. My dad points to a house across the street. "My uncle used to live there," he says. We haven't spent much time in Saint-Léonard-d'Aston before, and I've certainly never walked around the village.

We walk into the town hall and ring the bell. "We aren't really strong on history," the receptionist tells me after I explain what I'm after.

While I'm not paying attention, my dad floats away toward the desk where locals inquire about permits and zoning. There are a few people there. He's still on a bit of a high from the *fromagerie* and starts telling them about the history of poutine. "We were just at the old *fromagerie* and looking around where I used to make cheese curds. We're looking into it for the poutine story," he explains.

There's laughter, and one woman rolls her eyes, but most get involved in the conversation. This small town was a very small part of something much bigger, they agree. A grizzled old woman in the back of the room who had stayed quiet begins to pipe in with her version of the history of poutine. She delivers the script about Drummondville and Warwick nearly flawlessly. "We don't know where it started," she says definitively, in what she clearly intended to be the conclusion to this whole affair.

It's not. Some workers have come out from the back and have been listening. All of a sudden, the locals waiting in line, the old woman, the receptionist and the rest of the town staff begin arguing about who invented poutine and which story is most credible. I look at my dad and smile. He shrugs. We slowly head for the exit, leaving behind a crowd deep in debate.

"Do you want to go to where I had my first poutine?"

My dad's question catches me by surprise. "Yes. Of course. Where?" There had been a mention of the clay racing track, but we'd left that behind in our driving. We grab two cups of coffee from a drive-through as we head up the black ribbon of Highway 55. We don't really need the caffeine after the day's excitement, but it's part of the routine now.

About five minutes south of Saint-Grégoire on the banks of the St. Lawrence River, we pull into a local waste dump and an overgrown gravel parking lot. Dad steps out of the car and surveys the area. There's not much to look at. "It used to be here," he says. Much has changed over the past half century, and there's little clue left that this was once a clay racing track, where *les gars de la terre battue* piloted their stock cars and battled for local glory.

After a few seconds of knitting his brows and pacing, he's determined that the tall tree in the distance was once near the track's first turn. The tree must be centuries old. A few hundred metres beyond it, a farmer drives his tractor in a furrowed field. The farmer is near where the track's backstretch once stood. This small field may be one of the first places poutine was doled out to the gathered masses.

"I had my first poutine after the races were finished," my dad tells me, still looking out over the field and wondering. He explained how he and his friends got into his Chevy Impala one day after cheering for the victors and went in search of a snack, having been told there was a fry truck nearby serving something new.

There's now a modern six-lane highway not too far away, with a constant churn of large trucks rumbling down the blacktop. Where there were once race cars and crowds, only farmers' fields and abandoned industrial sites remain.

My father smiles as he looks around. "This chip wagon, which had been selling hot dogs and hamburgers near the races, decided to start offering poutine. People just threw themselves at it. Poutine became known really quickly after that. This is it for me," he says.

The exact year of that first poutine would become a running debate between the two of us for years. Initially, he was adamant that it had happened in 1964. That quickly proved an impossible date. Not only was that the same year the Roy Jucep opened, but a search of local newspapers and municipal records found no racetrack operating. Maybe 1966, before he had the car accident that sent him to Montreal's Notre Dame Hospital for nearly two weeks? Still too early, I'd tell him. The nearby Laviolette Bridge seems old now after spanning the river for more than a generation, especially given that it's covered in rust and bits of metal slapped onto the superstructure like patches on an old pair of jeans, but it only opened in 1967, a few days before Christmas. The bridge was standing during his first poutine, he remembers that much. Eventually we are left with 1971, one year after the track first opened, and the evening Dad witnessed the rivalry of the local Tessier brothers as they raced around the track.

The races were held every Sunday, starting after Saint-Jean-Baptiste Day and ending just before the first snowfall. Most of the racers were locals, representing Drummondville, Victoriaville and villages like Saint-Léonard-d'Aston. When races weren't on, people snuck onto the track to race their family cars or old beaters. Those very unsanctioned races usually followed an evening of drinking and boasting between friends, with the empty cans of a few six-packs rattling around on the back seat during a speedy joyride. My dad remembers piloting his Chevy Impala ss around the track. The "Super Sport" convertible had a big v8 engine and threw up clouds of dust from the clay. Every inch of the car was full of his friends, men and women, who were yelling at him to go faster. After a night of drinking, they ran rings around the circuit until the engine was steaming. "We didn't crash," he quickly adds.

The half-mile track opened in September 1970 with what was then dubbed the longest race in Canada, running for three hundred laps. Admission was initially $3.50, with a flyer for the race promising "action, emotion and thrill" on the track. The stands had room for three thousand people, but with the large city of Trois-Rivières just across the river, many more could show up for races on a sunny day.

"The Trois-Rivières racetrack could become the most popular and modern theatre for stock-car racing in Quebec," the local *Courrier Riviera* newspaper reported in a burst of optimism in 1970. That first race saw over four thousand people in the stands. It would remain a lively track for its first decade. Drivers from nearby towns, like the Tessier brothers, would nurture fan followings that came out to see them. In the 1970s, Nicolet local Léo Courchesne parachuted onto the track as a form of entertainment during a race. Well, almost. His chute got stuck on a track light and he was suspended above the tarmac for some time before a crew could get him down.

Pictures from the early 1970s show an area that's vastly different from the one I'm looking at with my dad. There are no farms and no trees—except for the one giant still standing today. The dirt track is surrounded by a white wooden fence. Spectators are sitting on their parked rides, watching the action. However, most of the thousands of people watching the race are in a long grandstand, a sea of humanity behind speeding metal.

Soon after that first three-hundred-lap race, the Descôteaux family *fromagerie* chose to try selling the new dish coming out of Drummondville. Armed with poutines, the Descôteaux fry truck quickly became a beacon for locals following the races. This is the era, as best as we can tell, where my dad showed up with his friends. They found the large gravel parking lot outside the *fromagerie* quickly becoming a zoo.

"Poutine, *le grand public*, everyone loved it," my dad tells me as we walk back to his car, the memories of those race days warming his words. "Not a lot of restaurants made it then. You could get it in Drummondville and maybe Victoriaville, but this was my first."

The visit to the site of his first poutine had given me another thread to follow. "You mentioned earlier that you might know someone connected to that poutine?" I ask.

"I know a guy I can call," my dad tells me. "He's a Descôteaux, the same family that owned the *fromagerie*. Let me look." He pulls out a small notepad he often carries—it's full of phone numbers and other reminders etched hurriedly over the years. He finds the number for Dany Descôteaux, who now lives in Trois-Rivières. I give the number a call and soon learn that over fifty years later, the Descôteaux family still serves up a good poutine.

Dany was only a toddler when his father and grandfather started dishing out bowls of poutine near the racetrack. His father had served my dad that first poutine, all those years ago. Dany is immediately enthusiastic on the phone and tells us to come by the Patachou, the restaurant he runs with his wife. We get into the car and head for the Laviolette Bridge—our poutine drive is finally bringing us back home.

"Poutine really is my family's story," Descôteaux tells me after we sit down at a booth in his restaurant. The Patachou feels like a 1950s diner that has fallen into a comic book—the walls are bright shades of red, yellow and blue. My dad and I are sitting on a black vinyl bench, and I spot a stuffed Fred Flintstone on the far wall. Despite a clientele that appears to be largely septuagenarian, the decor seems more Chuck E. Cheese. "I love comic books," Descôteaux tells me by way of explanation when I ask.

Cups of coffee for the three of us materialize seemingly out of nowhere, with cream and sugar. "At first it was my father, my grandfather, my aunts and uncles," he continues with his story. "We've been selling poutine since 1971. It's been around me nearly my whole life, but I've shown some self-restraint because I never got too big." He leans over and taps my father on his ample stomach. Descôteaux is the kind of man who can do that and get away with it. My father is the kind of man who would think it's funny.

Dad shrugs and winks. "Yes, I've eaten a lot of poutine," he says with a snort. The two men have also know each other for about a decade, crossing paths often in this corner of Trois-Rivières, near where I grew up.

The Descôteaux family made cheese and churned out butter for decades, stocking local pantries on the south side of the St. Lawrence River. The family's *fromagerie* stood on what is now Descôteaux Avenue, a quick drive from the long-gone racetrack. The factory had started life as a local co-operative in the 1940s, before Descôteaux's great-grandfather took it private during a rough patch. It was in a prime location, close to two main highways and lots of traffic.

Things were on a roll for the family and their first restaurant, in the form of a chip wagon that opened in the *fromagerie*'s parking lot in 1971. It was a hit, and soon the family converted it into a full dining establishment, the original Patachou. Though it was the same name as a popular Parisian cabaret singer of the era, the restaurant's moniker is also a pun based on something odd Descôteaux's dad was doing with his main dish. Along with the three main ingredients in poutine, he was also sprinkling cabbage on top, or in French, *patate et chou*. "I spent my youth waiting tables and talking with patrons. The kitchen was my playpen," Descôteaux tells us.

We take a sip of our coffees and my dad leans forward. "We're here to talk about those early years. We just spent the day driving across the river and we were at the old racetrack. We'd go to those races in Saint-Grégoire and then we'd stop at the fry shack run by your family. That was my first poutine," he tells Descôteaux. "We want to know more about that." The restaurant owner is nodding along to the explanation of why we're sitting in the Patachou with him.

"Okay, here's what I know," he says.

"We were close enough to Drummondville and all those small *fromageries* that put squeaky cheese curds in a poutine, so it wasn't really seen as something bizarre. But with a *fromagerie* of our own, the family also didn't immediately jump into building a restaurant.

"My grandfather just spent a lot of time going to nearby events early on. All the expositions and festivals he could find. My grandmother and grandfather did so many of those that they were just fed up with them, just completely fed up," Descôteaux tells us.

Not unlike a dairy farm of the era, or a family-owned convenience store today, the Descôteaux *fromagerie* put everyone to work. Descôteaux's father started working in the factory while he was still in elementary school, putting in a few hours daily from the day he turned eight years old. His younger uncles would sit down in the evenings and pack two or three thousand small bags of cheese curds for the family to sell the next day. "They'd just be told to sit down, get to work and finish so they could get to bed," he says.

The big turning point for the family's creamery was the construction of the Laviolette Bridge. The only span between Montreal and Quebec City, the busy bridge has a long, graceful arch and soars into the sky to allow ship traffic on the St. Lawrence River to continue unimpeded into the seaway and to the Great Lakes beyond. Its completion in 1967 opened up the family's business to a much larger base of customers—previously, their business had been limited by the slow ferry crossing.

Sophie Marcotte, Descôteaux's wife, walks over and chimes in. She works as a waitress at the restaurant and has just dropped off a load of plates at a neighbouring table. "Your grandmother told me that when they'd cross the river, before the bridge was built, they'd spend the day going back and forth on the ferry with little bags of curds to sell to motorists crossing."

With the bridge open, motorists could easily travel to visit the *fromagerie*. Descôteaux doesn't remember his father complaining of any trouble convincing Trifluvians, as the city's residents are called, to come across and try their wares. "Not at all. After the bridge opened, people would spend the next few years driving across it and ending up in front of my grandfather's *fromagerie*. They'd see the sign and eventually try a poutine," he says. Trois-Rivières's significant blue-collar population meant its residents were less resistant than those in the capital to a new dish popping up with squeaky cheese and a parochial image.

As a child, Descôteaux didn't spend much time in the neigh-bouring *fromagerie* since he was usually working in the restaurant. "I remember the odour though. It was memorable. It always smelled like curdled milk, and they didn't have good ventilation like today. The smell just hung around," he tells us.

My dad agrees and adds a story from his time in the creamery. "The quality of the milk wasn't like today. I once got to the *fromagerie* and there was a cat in the jug I'd been carrying on my truck. You know, cats like milk," he says matter-of-factly. "The farmer must have put the jug out and didn't put the cover on right away. And the cat must have jumped up to start drinking the milk and fell in. I guess the cat was at the bottom of the jug and the farmer never saw it when he put the cover firmly on it. I got the jug to the creamery and started emptying it. That gave me quite the fright!"

"Was it dead?" I ask him, riveted.

"Of course it was dead. The damned thing drowned in the milk," he tells us. Descôteaux is hanging off every word.

"If you'd already been pouring the milk out, did you make cheese with that batch of milk?" I ask him.

"Hmm. I don't remember."

The Descôteaux clan operated the cheese factory and neighbouring restaurant for a decade, but things changed as Descôteaux's grandfather approached retirement age. "In 1981, my grandfather sold the business because my father had no interest in taking over the *fromagerie*. My father lived his entire bloody life in the place and he said he'd had enough. He went into running his restaurant full time. Later that year, he crossed the St. Lawrence River and started building another restaurant in Trois-Rivières."

The timing was fortunate. Despite its early popularity, the racetrack on the south shore wouldn't last. Only fifteen years after it opened, the track's owner closed it for the last time. "We've been open for fifteen years, we've had problems for fifteen years," Jacques Lambert told a local newspaper in 1986. "It was built two miles too far to the south." Two miles to the north would put the track in a busy suburb of Trois-Rivières near the new Descôteaux restaurant.

Other than yellowed newspaper clippings and largely forgotten races, little exists but my father's memories of that first poutine—and the memories of the thousands of others who joined him in discovering the dish there. The track sits at the very northern limit of the Centre-du-Québec region where we've done so much of our driving. Across the St. Lawrence River, Trois-Rivières sits in its own region, the Mauricie. Canada's second-oldest city, it was a very different domain from its rural cousin to the south when the races were still on. At the time, it was dominated by pulp and paper, forestry work and a vibrant garment industry. Sitting midway between Montreal and Quebec City on the province's busiest highway, Trois-Rivières would be a new toehold, after the provincial capital, for poutine outside of its rural heartland.

At that point, Marcotte comes over and fills our coffee cups. She also drops some menus in front of us and smiles at her husband. "Let them order something when you're done talking," she says, lightly teasing him.

"How did your family first get the idea for poutine?" I ask Descôteaux.

He frowns. "I'm not sure," he says, pulling out his phone. He starts calling up aunts to ask them about the family history. There's a lot of back and forth. My father and I just sit there, listening to one side of the conversation. I sip my coffee. Every few minutes my dad will hear something come across and chime in: "No, not that one" or "That restaurant wasn't open yet." Calls are swapped and dropped as the phone tree grows. But a cohesive narrative eventually starts to form, and they collectively tell him that the idea likely came from a nearby restaurant in Nicolet called Ti-Boss. The small diner was about eight kilometres away from the racetrack in the opposite direction from the Patachou. To me, the name brings to mind the history of the Roy Jucep and the chef they called Ti-Pout—but that would be way too much of a coincidence. I'd later learn that the Ti-Boss closed years ago and the location was bought by a local chain called Stratos. With the Ti-Boss closed, that part of poutine's greater story has since grown very cold.

Sipping his coffee, my dad gets excited when he hears the name Ti-Boss, literally *little boss* in Québécois slang. He knows the place: "We'd go to the bar and afterwards, when we were pretty drunk, we'd all drive down to the Ti-Boss for some poutine. We'd take the Saint-Esprit road to get there," my dad says. "And you really needed the Holy Spirit to get there safe after all the drinking."

Those boozy late-night food runs to Ti-Boss happened in the years after that first poutine at the racetrack, but they confirm that poutine was quickly establishing itself in the restaurants and stomachs of the region. (It's worth noting that cultural norms and the enforcement of the laws around drunk driving have shifted tremendously in Quebec, and more widely across Canada, in the decades since those questionable drives.)

"I would never say we invented it—that's a distinction that doesn't belong to us—but we brought poutine across the river to Trois-Rivières," Descôteaux says as we get back on track. His family is proud of the small role it played. "We helped popularize it. We helped bring it out of the regions and into the cities. We eventually owned seven restaurants in the Mauricie—we certainly helped make it popular."

For the record, Descôteaux has always thought that the Roy Jucep invented poutine. He dismissed the "little discord" between Drummondville and other local towns as largely irrelevant today. "Look, everyone makes poutine now. That's not the point anymore. Even other Canadians are making it now," he tells me.

Descôteaux is surprised, however, to learn how much poutine has spread in English Canada today, appearing in food courts and on many restaurant menus. "It's a bigger Canadian food now? Wow. I really thought it was mostly a Quebec thing," he says. After a moment of reflection, he adds that he's happy other Canadians are getting to enjoy his favourite dish. But then a question comes to him. "Check out the cheese, that's what's important to me. Is it cheese curds and are they fresh?" I tell him it's possible the cheese isn't always fresh. He reserves judgment anyway. "Well, they've got to work with what they've got, I guess."

We turn back to the Patachou's history in Quebec. Locally, the restaurant's influence extended beyond the kitchen. For a long time, residents in Trois-Rivières called a poutine a "patachou" when ordering, after the restaurant where they'd first tasted it. The name fell out of fashion in the late 1980s as poutine became increasingly standardized. But in recent years, Descôteaux has added the patachou name for poutine back to the menu with a note on its history.

Unlike some of the teething problems it faced in Quebec City, poutine was a quick hit in Trois-Rivières, and the Descôteaux family was the first to put the dish on the menu locally. Within a decade, Descôteaux's father had opened his seven restaurants across the Mauricie region. One thing that didn't survive was the cabbage-topped poutine that helped give the restaurant its name. "People just didn't like it," he tells us. It was quietly dropped. No one has tried to order one in decades, Descôteaux tells me.

With the family business growing in the 1980s, Descôteaux went off to college to study drawing. He wasn't around as his father's collection of restaurants went into decline. The family had spent too much money expanding too quickly. By the time Descôteaux was back in Trois-Rivières and wanted to take over the family business, the Patachou was down to two locations. He and his wife operate the remaining restaurant.

Today, Descôteaux's biggest challenge is balancing his family life with the daily demands of making so much poutine. He's been with his wife for two decades and they have two children. "If my kids want to take over someday, we'll let them, but we're aiming for them to be accountants or neurosurgeons. We'll accept notary or lawyer," he says with a smile.

"Plumber or electrician," his wife yells from across the restaurant, where she's been keeping an ear on the conversation.

"But not restaurants," they both add at the same time.

With more than ninety thousand customers annually, the Patachou turns out a lot of poutine. Descôteaux doesn't keep statistics like some of the larger diners, but he knows his potato order. He brings in 150 bags of potatoes weekly, each weighing about seven kilograms. An ocean of gravy and daily shipments of curds are added to it all. His poutines are simple. The most popular is the classic, with a spicy gravy and fresh cheese curds. Some of his regulars order their poutine with the more traditional BBQ-style gravy and he'll dish that up instead. Another poutine recipe, covered in spaghetti sauce, is beloved by other patrons.

Facing growing competition, he's putting up a fight by doubling down on poutine. He now has fourteen variations on offer, from the bacon and onions of the Pantheon poutine to the carrots and mushrooms of the Gardiner. To celebrate a half century of operations, Descôteaux also brought back a retro poutine modelled on his father's dish from the 1970s. It's made from frozen fries and is served in a styrofoam bowl.

"Someone sent me a photo of a man who is terminally ill, and his last family photo is here, with everyone gathered around and eating poutines out of foam bowls. What surprised me wasn't just all the sympathies under the photo, but all the questions from people about where the man got the poutine in the foam bowl," Descôteaux says, referring to the post online. The retro dish has been a hit.

Descôteaux explains that despite all the additional choices on his menu, everything still revolves around the classic poutine. Even so, he doesn't shun some of the fancier fare to come out of Montreal's food scene, where poutine has been dressed up with expensive ingredients. "It's a long way from where it started. It adds gastronomy to it. I don't want to denigrate poutine, but it's really just gravy, fries and cheese after all. But what those guys are doing in Montreal helps bring poutine to another level. I appreciate that, but not here," he says. "My clientele is very steak and potatoes."

My dad is nodding in approval. He hasn't been here very often, but he likes what he's hearing. The restaurant is starting to fill up around us as we talk. There are green salads and gourmet paninis on the menu, but the well-thumbed pages are in the middle with the poutines.

While there's been a push for healthier items in recent years, that hasn't affected poutine sales. A large number of patrons come back, day after day, for a poutine. Even a recent move toward breakfast, with more options on the early morning menu, has been anchored by a growing selection of breakfast poutines. Why not start the day with fries, eggs, hollandaise sauce and grated cheese?

Descôteaux invites us back to his kitchen to help him throw together a few poutines for customers. It's a tight space, but after a lifetime in the kitchen, he's barely looking as he grabs a basket of fries and stirs the gravy. He's in his element and at ease. Bubbles pop on the surface of the large vat of brown sauce while the fries are boiling away. I can't keep up as he moves gracefully around us. "Which poutine would you like?" Descôteaux asks, having sent three dishes out to the floor over the past five minutes.

"The retro poutine!" my dad answers quickly. "I haven't had that one. I'd like to try a taste of the good old days."

Descôteaux smiles and gets to work, dumping more fries into the oil and giving his sauce a stir. I tiptoe over to give it a covert smell and a rich wave of soothing gravy aroma greets me. "It's an old recipe," Descôteaux says with a smile.

He tells us to stand back as our poutine is nearly ready. The styrofoam bowl, narrow with high sides, is set on a wooden counter and filled with golden brown fries. He grabs a large handful of cheese curds and mixes them in. Then he stops. "This is when it comes together," he says, picking up a large metal ladle and scooping up the sauce. There are bits of pepper floating on the top as he tips it over the poutine, slowly filling the bowl and letting the gravy trickle to the bottom. He ushers us back to the booth where we'd been talking earlier.

Let's clear one thing up: by this point, we've eaten a lot of poutine on our journey into poutine's history. We haven't consulted a medical professional, but it's an amount that likely far exceeds any recommended dose. Yet my father's stomach, which is rapidly approaching its eightieth birthday, is still going strong. "You go first," I tell him. He needs no further encouragement.

Descôteaux's poutine looks gorgeous, and the incredibly climate-unfriendly styrofoam bowl does a great job as I pass it over to my dad. Without a word, he dives in and takes his first bite. He gives me a thumbs-up as he goes for another forkful—this apparently won't be a take-turns experience. I take advantage of a momentary lull in his pumping steam shovel to get a bite. It's very good. The experience brings out an orchestra of sounds. The golden fries crunch without being dry, the cheese squeaks loudly and the gravy ties it all together. Descôteaux's classic would be a strong contender in any poutine battle.

I hadn't come to Patachou with very high expectations. My dad had never mentioned the restaurant or Descôteaux before he dropped that "I know a guy" line while staring at an empty farmer's field. I also grew up a few blocks away from where we are sitting and must have driven past this little roadside pop of colour, at the edge of a greying, post-industrial city, a few hundred times during my youth without noticing it. It's nice to discover something new and wonderful. Decades after it first started dishing out poutines, the Patachou is still around, and a Descôteaux is still at the helm. It's one of the few links still going all the way back to poutine's early days outside of Drummondville.

After saying our goodbyes to Dany and Sophie, we get back into my dad's car and start the short drive back to his house. The last rays of sunshine are coming down and this first part of our journey, scouting the early days of poutine, is coming to an end. In Drummondville, Warwick, Princeville and Quebec City we've met characters who illuminated where the dish was born and the chance encounters that made it happen. The next chapter now lies to the west, away from poutine's rural heartland and toward bigger cities and gourmet dining. My dad won't be coming along physically on this part of the poutine journey—the price of admission is driving to Montreal, and that's too high.

I ask him again if he'd like to change his mind.

"The aggressive drivers, the busy traffic, the narrow roads. No, thank you," he says. But he's just a quick call away, and this voyage of discovery is nowhere near done.

"What do you want for dinner?" he asks me, more from habit than hunger.

"Poutine?" I say.

He replies with an exaggerated groan. "I think I'll be eating a diet of lettuce and radish for the next few days."

Poutine's beating heart: La Banquise

THERE'S NEARLY ALWAYS A LINEUP OUTSIDE LA BANQUISE IN Montreal on a sunny day. And on a rainy day. And a snowy day. During the heat of summer, the line can stretch down Rachel Street into the city's busy Plateau neighbourhood. Lineups aren't all that unusual in the area, with a number of trendy bars and restaurants nearby where queues are to be expected. The foot traffic is heavy with all types. The restaurant is also located close to one of the city's favourite parks, La Fontaine, where a steady procession of friends and lovers walk to a small lake and its large fountain for a break from the summer heat.

Despite the expected wait in the area, the lineup at La Banquise is generally unlike the others. What sets La Banquise apart are the patrons. Mixed in with the locals are a great many tourists, who often seem confused by the long queue and end up weaving into the busy street and the path of oncoming cyclists, who ding angrily. If the would-be diners have escaped Canada's fairly diligent approach to lining up before this moment, La Banquise is where the lesson will be driven home. The local custom of not cutting in line, not trying to squeak through, is rigidly enforced by others. Not that it's often needed as the lineup is generally a happy one. And why wouldn't it be? The foodies and average travellers standing in the Montreal sun are now only steps from what's been promised as an authentic experience.

It's clear from the hastily picked-up French words and comfortable English phrases heard in the line that many of these tourists come from around the world. On the day I joined the queue outside La Banquise, quite a few were American, as large families and standing apart as couples, often wearing the logos of rival sports teams and colleges found south of the border. Regardless of where they started out, they are now all united by the quest for cheese curds, fries and gravy. Amid the polyglot clamour of the crowd, one word breaks through: poutine.

It's likely that no restaurant has done more to expose the wider world to poutine in the past few decades than La Banquise. It certainly didn't invent or popularize poutine, and it would be a stretch to claim that it has improved upon the basic dish. But what it has is a solid plate of poutine in a place where tourists can easily find it.

Years after the late American chef Anthony Bourdain salivated over five different plates of poutine in the restaurant during the filming of one of his television shows, calling the dish a "thoroughly wonderful gastronomic train wreck," people still come to La Banquise looking for the emotion he brought to poutine. "I feel so dirty, yet so alive," Bourdain beamed, fork at the ready. There's no way to watch the pleasure of Bourdain digging into a plate of poutine and not smile. For tourists who have never heard of Drummondville and won't leave the comforts of the island of Montreal, this is likely the closest they'll get to a poutine with history. And it's here they'll get down and dirty with the curds.

Poutine's early years in Montreal are shrouded in mystery, and much of what's already been published, which is very little, appears to be wrong. Suggested dates in general culinary histories that claim the 1980s and later for poutine's arrival are far too late and based on nothing obvious. What is clear is that there was no triumphant arrival of poutine in the metropolis where so much of Quebec lives. Instead of a tickertape parade, poutine faced decades of stigmatization by English Montrealers and their cultural institutions before it became an indelible part of the city's landscape.

Pierre Barsalou's path to poutine wasn't exactly predictable. He didn't grow up to be a chef or a restaurateur. Instead, he was sitting in a fire hall in 1968, still a young man and only six years into what would be a long career as a firefighter. He was contemplating a dream to sell ice cream while keeping his day job at Montreal's Number 16 firehall. It's an old and classically handsome building at the corner of Rachel Street and Christopher Columbus Avenue, across from La Fontaine Park. However, his ruminations about fire and ice were soon interrupted by an alarm. Along with the smell of smoke came an opportunity in the form of a fire just across the street from the fire hall. A rental sign was soon hung on the small commercial storefront damaged by the flames. Barsalou walked across Rachel and signed a lease. La Banquise, named after the pack ice you can find bobbing on the St. Lawrence River in the depths of a frigid winter, was born in May 1968.

The Plateau neighbourhood of Barsalou's restaurant was the one then being immortalized by Mordecai Richler in *The Apprenticeship of Duddy Kravitz* and *St. Urbain's Horseman*. Often working-class and gritty, it was home to waves of immigrants to Montreal, especially members of the city's Jewish population. While much of the French and English middle class had left for newer areas of the city, there still remained a large French-speaking presence in the Plateau's east where the restaurant stood. Quebec playwright Michel Tremblay captured the more francophone character of the streets immediately around the fire hall itself. Long before the Plateau became a lively cultural hub, the area's hard-up residents weren't exactly a strong client base to support Barsalou's plans. Undaunted, he got to work that first summer selling ice cream, with the park ensuring he had enough customers to empty his freezer.

As the temperature started falling in late 1968, the newly minted restaurant owner had already detected a fatal flaw in his ice cream shop: there's little demand for ice cream in the middle of a Montreal winter and the rent still comes due. It was time for a change of course. To better understand what came next, I spoke with Barsalou's daughter Annie. She was the co-owner of La Banquise with her husband, Marc Latendresse, when I reached her on the phone while researching poutine's arrival in Montreal.

La Banquise spent that first winter in hibernation before reopening with tubs of ice cream the next summer. Barsalou had used his time off to hatch a new plan. In the fall of 1969, the small ice cream shop transformed itself into that classic Quebec institution: a *casse-croûte*. "He figured he'd open an around-the-clock snack shop, which worked with his hours as a firefighter. As a firefighter you work shifts, and on the Plateau, life is pretty much twenty-four hours a day. So he dove into that idea, with just fries and hot dogs at the start," Annie explains.

Instead of catering solely to locals, Barsalou had found a market that he understood well and had correctly identified as being underserved. His patrons became fellow firefighters, emergency crews, taxi drivers and the clientele who spilled out of local bars at closing time. All people who either work or want to eat outside of regular hours. While he kept ice cream and milkshakes during the day, the menu slowly expanded over time to cater to that late crowd, with rotisserie chicken, sandwiches and shepherd's pie being added. Despite the changes, it remained a firefighter's snack bar and a home for night owls,

Annie says—a place where Barsalou served what he himself wanted to eat.

These were lean times for poutine. In the early 1970s, Ashton Leblond in Quebec City was struggling to get locals to sample anything with cheese curds. The Descôteaux family was doing better, selling poutine outside of Trois-Rivières, but they were a small satellite operating at the edge of the Centre-du-Québec region where poutine was born.

The social stigma that came with sampling a rural dish, which was so pervasive in Quebec City in those early days, would be doubly so in Montreal. The linguistic tensions running through the city added to it, with English Montrealers eventually holding poutine up as a symbol of a perceived French-Canadian lack of sophistication. Was Montreal's first poutine served at La Banquise? "Likely not, but it must have been close to first," Annie tells me. "There was almost none in Montreal at the time, that's all I know."

Barsalou had unwittingly created the perfect toehold for poutine in Montreal. It included a late-night crowd that was harried and looking for a quick snack during a long shift. It was largely French-speaking, so it wouldn't be put off by something from Drummondville or Warwick. Either way, it was very Québécois. Most importantly, the average patron wouldn't have a deeply rooted pretentiousness that caused them to turn their nose up at a sloppy mess of a dish. Many restaurants would be too English, too downtown or too set in their ways to strike out on something as odd as poutine. Not La Banquise. All it needed was a spark, and that came either in 1977 or 1979—the records and the people with memory of the event aren't exactly sure which.

"The idea came from a waitress who was on vacation and visited her family in the Centre-du-Québec region," Annie explains over the phone. "She ate poutine at a snack bar. When she came back, she told my dad about it. Because we already had fries and sauce on the menu, all we'd need to add was the cheese curds. My dad thought it was a good idea, so he put in an order for cheese curds. We started with the classic poutine and the Italian poutine, which came covered in spaghetti sauce."

It's not clear where the waitress picked up her first plate of poutine, but it was likely somewhere on the poutine highway between Drummondville and Princeville.

The new classic poutine was a hit with the reliable crew of regulars at La Banquise. However, in a city with a rich local cuisine like Montreal's, poutine didn't make much of an early splash. In the increasingly bohemian Plateau neighbourhood alone, La Banquise was competing with the iconic bagels at St-Viateur, the lunch counter at Wilensky's and the smoked meat sandwiches from Schwartz's—an incredible set of iconic foods all within an easy fifteen-minute walk. In the wider city, other memorable dishes were also gaining a following. The Orange Julep, housed in a three-storey orange-shaped structure off a major highway, had opened for Expo 67 and was attracting motorists. Farther north, a small burger stand called Dic Ann's was helping popularize fast food. Both would become renowned local eateries. Back in the Plateau, Barsalou stuck with what he had and began setting the foundation for what would eventually become Montreal's grandest institution for poutine.

Still a firefighter, Barsalou moved to the suburbs and got to work starting a family. Eventually, his daughters began spending time in the kitchen with him, cleaning dishes and waiting on tables. Annie's life slowly but invariably headed toward the trade. She took courses in hospitality and learned how to run a restaurant by the book. But first, she rolled up her sleeves and helped out when she could.

In addition to its arrival in Montreal, poutine was slowly emerging into the national consciousness. It was seen outside of its rural hinterland as a mixture that was confusing, backward, embarrassing and quite exotic. The indisputably positive reviews were few. The dish first appeared in the pages of *The Globe and Mail* in 1982, described to the national paper's largely Ontario audience as a "plate of mystery" found in Quebec. The blips on the cultural radar appear with growing frequency in the mid-1980s and often speak of poutine as an oddity.

One of the more contentious characterizations came in the pages of Montreal's *Gazette* in 1987, when the political cartoonist Aislin put the English community's view of poutine into the community's paper of record. He suggested that poutine was "the most horrible culinary disaster of the twentieth century"—worse, he ventured, than haggis. It's hard to imagine a lower point for poutine in the metropolis and in the anglophone community. It was now known enough among regular readers to be a punchline for embarrassment.

Reading about Montreal's English community punching down on poutine left me with a sour taste in my mouth. Luckily, that's when my dad called.

"Hello, mister. So what's new with poutine?" he asked. I told him some of what I'd learned about La Banquise. "Never heard of it," he interjected.

"It's a big restaurant in Montreal, I promise," I told him. "But while I've got you on the phone, what do you know about the word *poutine*? Did you ever use it to mean a mess?" I was looking further into the origin of the word and thinking about that "*maudite poutine*" quip from Warwick back in 1957, when Fernand Lachance used it to mean a bloody mess.

There were a few moments of silence while he thought it over. "I've never used it that way, but I think that's how people used to use it. You should ask Descôteaux," he told me.

So I messaged Dany Descôteaux and asked what he thought about the etymology of poutine and its messy origin. "That's what I've always heard, but I'm not sure," he messaged back.

Thankfully, it wasn't long before I came upon an unexpected source of linguistic clarity. It was deep in the musty archives of Quebec's National Assembly, from the minutes of debates of the era. The first recorded use of the word *poutine* logged in the archives, after that first Warwick dish was served in 1957, was uttered in 1965 by Quebec conservative leader and soon-to-be premier Daniel Johnson Sr. He called a complicated rail deal being negotiated by the Liberal governments in Quebec City and Ottawa a "poutine" during debate. He clearly meant from context that it was a mess, and there was no note in the record explaining the meaning. René Lévesque soon began using the word as well. Powered by Lévesque's oratory, poutine began appearing increasingly often in the public record, as politicians on both sides started slinging verbal "poutines" at each other. In 1982, Liberal Michel Gratton let on that the word was gaining new meaning when, in a debate with Lévesque, he deadpanned that the "Liberal poutine is being replaced by the Péquiste ratatouille."

If that wink toward food wasn't clear enough, Gilles Richard, a representative for the province's wildlife council, told legislators in 1982 that they should leave the big cities and go to rural areas with "restaurants that sell poutines" to better understand hunting and fishing. It's clear from the records that people knew what he was talking about and that poutine was considered a reasonable way to distinguish town from country. If poutine was available in Montreal in 1982, beyond La Banquise, it was so uncommon as to not even register as an urban dish. The second Chez Ashton location had only just opened in Quebec City a few months earlier.

By 1990, poutine was increasingly and explicitly being used in Quebec's halls of power as a shorthand for the province's rural regions, but that original "messy" meaning was still holding on in recorded debates as well. *Home Alone* and *Terminator 2* were in theatres, MC Hammer was all over the radio and American troops were soon to come home to a large victory parade at the end of the first Persian Gulf war. In Quebec, politicians were still accusing each other of being disastrously inept by being a bunch of "poutines." But the newer meaning was creeping in. During a debate on immigration, Benjamin Teitelbaum, then president of the Canadian Council for the Rights of Minorities, said it would be a "shock for immigrants who arrive in the regions and aren't necessarily used to, you know, in quotation marks, eating some poutine. You know?" You can imagine him throwing up his hands as he narrates the "quotation marks," with a barely concealed shiver at the evocation of poutine.

In the end, the real winner—the first politician to talk about poutine as a food in the province's National Assembly—is Gil Rémillard. And it's a doozy. The word came up during a debate in May 1992 on the state of constitutional negotiations with Ottawa. A national referendum on reforming Canada's constitution was only months away. Rémillard, then the province's justice minister, brought up poutine as a symbol of how Quebec isn't unique during a debate on whether the province should be considered a distinct society in a revised constitution. "After all, we are not distinct because of our poutine, Mr. Speaker, especially after I learned recently that poutine comes from New Brunswick and not Quebec. It isn't by putting a cherry on a poutine that you have a sundae. That's evident," he said, in what should go down as one of the most perfidious and bewildering errors uttered in the chamber's history.

We can perhaps forgive Rémillard for his loose grasp of poutine fact as he was in the midst of grinding constitutional negotiations while simultaneously rewriting the province's entire legal code. His error can likely be traced to a traditional Acadian dish from the Maritimes called *poutine râpée*. It's a boiled potato dumpling usually filled with salted pork. While it's delicious and shares a similar name, the Maritime dish lacks the fries, gravy and cheese curds of a poutine. How Quebec's top lawyer could confuse the two is troubling. Rémillard was never asked to retract and apologize for what was hopefully just very poor staff work. There's still time to set the record right.

The classic junk food of that era wasn't poutine. It was hot dogs. During one of the constant arguments between Quebec and the federal government during the 1970s and '80s, Prime Minister Pierre Trudeau grew increasingly impatient with Premier Robert Bourassa. Trudeau, in a moment of hot temper after Quebec passed its first language law, called the Quebec premier a classless kind of a guy, a *"mangeur de hot dog."* He couldn't think of a worse, more lowbrow thing to be associated with than eating hot dogs.

While you might not want your politicians mugging for the cameras with them, hot dogs were the junk food of choice in Montreal. A number of greasy spoon chains that still span the island of Montreal, like Lafleur, Valentine and La Belle Province, started up in the fifties and seventies with the express purpose of serving hot dogs.

One of the institutions from that era is the Montreal Pool Room. Despite the name, the restaurant doesn't have any pool tables today. Near the corner of Saint-Laurent Boulevard and Sainte-Catherine Street, it's right at the centre of what was once Montreal's thriving redlight district. Today, it's still a bit shabby, though the city is years into a long plan to push out the smut and replace it with offices and cultural venues. One of the few remaining strip clubs, the Café Cléopâtre, is across the street from the Montreal Pool Room.

One day in the fall I walk down to the area, not to explore its sultry past but to meet with McGill University's Daniel Béland. It quickly becomes clear to me that the Montreal Pool Room is still a favourite to many, with a colourful cast of characters coming through. It also does a brisk trade in hot dogs to this day. While I'm waiting for Béland to appear, a number of people are double-parked; they're pulling up, choking traffic on one of Montreal's busiest streets, to quickly pop in and grab a tray of hot dogs from the restaurant.

In a sign of the changing times, the Montreal Pool Room makes poutine now as well. The steamed hot dog remains their bestseller, but they've also got a poutine with homemade fries and gravy. I ask the man working the counter if it's good here. His reaction isn't encouraging. He turns and pulls a bag of cheese curds out of a freezer. "You be the judge," he says with a shrug, the cold condensation leaking on the bag. Béland admits after walking in a few minutes later that the poutine really isn't all that good, but he wanted to meet here because of the restaurant's history. He comes here for the feelings the place brings him.

"Poutine didn't exist here when I was a kid in the late 1970s and early 1980s," Béland tells me. "It's possible it was there, but I didn't encounter it." Béland came to the restaurant often when his dad worked in downtown Montreal for Hydro-Quebec. His office was only a short walk away, and the Pool Room was a nice place to bring your kid for a quick work lunch when they weren't in school.

Three decades later, the Montreal Pool Room hasn't changed much, he tells me. "It's a kind of iconic place for Montreal. But it's all about the hot dogs, and that's a much older tradition in Montreal than poutine culture. It's good to see that both now live well together." There's honking outside the restaurant—a man has just pulled up in an SUV and jumped out, blocking traffic on Saint-Laurent Boulevard. "Two steamies," he calls over to the counter. The honking just grows louder, as it has for decades in front of the Pool Room.

This is the state of poutine in the early 1990s—budding, but not quite arrived on the main stage of Montreal yet. Barsalou, father, firefighter, owner of La Banquise, was tired. In 1994, he sold the restaurant to his daughters. "La Banquise was looking a little threadbare when we took over," Annie tells me, nearly three decades after she bought half the place. She was only nineteen at the time and had just taken on something that her father had poured much of his life into. The restaurant had scuffed-up furniture and a floor showing years of abuse, with burn spots from numerous accidents and carelessly flicked cigarettes. The neighbourhood itself was in a rough patch after the remaining working-class population had started heading for the suburbs, leaving behind students and others attracted to the cheap rent.

The two sisters rolled up their sleeves and were officially in the restaurant business. They split nearly all the shifts, keeping La Banquise open around the clock for the night owls of the Plateau. The restaurant slowly underwent repairs and refurbishment during the 1990s. The two new owners also muddled through a lost decade for Quebec, as a second independence referendum in 1995 sent a wave of jobs and business out of Quebec toward Ontario. The economy entered a tailspin that would last well into the next millennium. In the final year of the 1990s, two major changes hit La Banquise. First, Annie's sister sold her shares in the restaurant to Annie's partner, Marc Latendresse, and left the business. Secondly, something peculiar happened: Elvis entered the building.

The poutine at La Banquise hadn't changed much in the decades since Barsalou helped introduce it to Montreal. It was the classic triumvirate, with fries, cheese and gravy. But something slowly started to change. "The idea for making poutines with all kinds of toppings came from our clients," Annie tells me. "One night a few guys came up to the counter and one of them asked for a poutine with different toppings. What did they want? Ground beef, peppers and mushrooms. I made it up and just put a price on it then and there. 'Wait a minute,' I thought, and I asked him, 'Do you want to name it?' I told him I'd put it on the menu right away and if it was popular I'd leave it on year-round. He called it the Elvis. He'd just watched the second Elvis Gratton film, and the light just went off in my head: 'This could really be a big thing.'"

Where would poutine be without its patrons? The dish likely never would have been invented without Eddy Lainesse's odd request back in the 1950s: "Just mix it all up in a bag." And now, a few late-night revellers had similarly come forward with another odd request. At La Banquise, it sent poutine in a new direction.

This was 1999. If you haven't heard of Elvis Gratton, you're likely not a Quebecer. Three movies and a TV series have been released based on the fictional character Bob Gratton, a clownish Québécois Elvis impersonator. They are classic Quebec fare now. Created by director Pierre Falardeau, who was also a vocal activist for Quebec's independence, the character was meant as political satire, with Elvis Gratton meant to represent what a disgusted Falardeau saw as the lazy, fat, American-loving Quebecers who had voted a few years earlier to remain in Canada. The satire didn't stick, and Gratton became a quotable cultural icon. After a night of knee-slapping fun at the movies, it's no surprise a few young diners wanted to honour Elvis Gratton with a poutine. Annie kept her promise and the Elvis is still on the menu.

Poutine was growing increasingly popular in Montreal by the late 1990s. A number of popular hot dog chains around the city added it to their menus. Slowly at first, and then quite rapidly, poutine became fully established throughout Montreal, even in English-speaking areas. Plenty of restaurants were now serving their version of the classic, and many menus also carried an Italian version of poutine, with chefs experimenting with the best spaghetti sauce to pour on fries and cheese. And with Chez Ashton in Quebec City adding two new permutations of poutine to its permanent menu, there was a smell of discovery in the air.

With the Elvis selling well, Annie sensed something that La Banquise could use to set itself apart from its growing number of competitors. "We started adding more poutines, with new additions every few months. Eventually, the number of poutines was completely outweighing the daily menu and we had to split them off. A year later we dropped the daily menu completely and focused solely on poutine. We quickly had thirty options and that became our calling. And that was that," she says with a sigh.

It was the early 2000s and, with its singular focus on poutine, La Banquise was on its way to being a Montreal landmark. The area around the restaurant was also slowly starting to clean up, with new shops taking over empty storefronts and cafés moving in to cater to the large student population spilling out from the areas around McGill and UQAM. One thing that stayed constant was La Banquise's determination to feed the customers that had supported it through the decades. The restaurant remains open twenty-four hours a day and emergency workers still come in droves.

"The Plateau-Mont Royal has evolved a lot, that's true, but people come from elsewhere in the city to this area. There aren't a lot of restaurants open around the clock anymore, but that's part of what sets us apart: we're always open, we're always there for you," she says.

The restaurant remains busy overnight. It's a crowded, jovial and shambolic place after dark. Along with the first responders and students, bar patrons still come in at 3 a.m. after their watering holes have started closing down. Then the exhausted staff from those bars come around at 5 a.m. for an after-work snack. With dawn just around the corner, the breakfast crowd isn't far behind.

Once bohemian and somewhat tattered, the Plateau has become one of Montreal's most sought-after neighbourhoods. Still vibrant with local culture and food, the area's once inexpensive student rentals are now being turned into family homes worth over a million. Annie isn't complaining about the increasing numbers of local tourists in the area—she's helped bring it about, judging by the long line outside.

The restaurant's poutine is still relatively cheap and close to being recession-proof, she says. "When the economy is doing well, people eat poutine. When the economy is doing poorly, people skip the fancier restaurants and eat poutine. We live through it all."

In 2023, La Banquise was purchased by Jean-Christophe Lirette and Émily Adam. The sale caused a ripple in Quebec's business pages, not because the Barsalou clan was selling what it had built but because of who was buying. A year earlier, Lirette and Adam had also purchased the Chez Ashton chain. One Montreal-based reporter described the sale as a "usurpation" of one of the city's chaotic and beloved institutions by a growing corporation based in the provincial capital.

Promises were made by the new owners, self-titled "magicians of poutine," that the restaurant would stay as it is and wouldn't be converted into an Ashton. Some changes are possible. A few months after buying out Ashton Leblond in a deal that was backed by two banks and a large union-controlled fund, the duo dropped the Chez from the name of that chain.

Despite the sale, the classic remains the bestseller at La Banquise, and the Elvis sits proudly near the top. The twenty-nine other poutines currently on the menu represent the promise of an incredible safari for your tastebuds. Along with gravy and cheese curds, there is a vast choice of concoctions with bits of hot dogs, corn dogs and smoked meat. Poring over the menu, a few stuck out at me. The Fred Flintstone tops a classic poutine with ground beef, smoked meat, bits of spicy sausage and merguez sausage. The Royal has pulled pork, boiled apple and bacon, while the Curfew includes ground beef, onions, cheese sauce and hot peppers, as well as mac 'n' cheese bites. It's quite a lot of choice.

Remaining alert to trends is also important for a restaurant that's constantly bringing in a new crowd. There's now a vegan option, with vegan curds and sauce. Workers and cooks are encouraged to strike up conversations with patrons, especially if those diners aren't stuffing their faces with glee. New ideas are always welcome. "Had we stayed with the same menu for the past twenty-eight years, or for the past fifty years, we wouldn't still be here today," Annie says.

Looking around, I see the laid-back appeal of La Banquise that's central to its identity. There's no uniform for the largely university-aged workers. Anything that's halfway decent is fine by Annie—not too dirty and not too many holes in a T-shirt will do. The crowds are thick, and the waiter bringing food to my table, weaving a path as best she can through a throng that just pushed through the front door, could best be described as snowboard-instructor-in-summer chic. The music, a mix of light pop and something more raucous, is the choice of someone working the floor right now. Neither of these are revolutionary ideas for a Montreal restaurant, but they put La Banquise in a different league from other corporate joints putting forward a more uniform image. I wrote in my notebook, a year before the sale, that La Banquise hasn't grown up and put a suit on yet, and it never will if it's to remain what it is. I remain convinced of that.

I ask Annie to walk me through the restaurant. The tables, chairs and walls are all popping with colour. "Our decor is the evolution of the restaurant over the last half century. It's modern while keeping some of the family cachet we've built over time. The benches for our booths are made out of blue leather with repurposed wood. The tables are covered with drawings from employees and their families. Each table has someone's personality. We've got photos on the walls and they come from an employee who was taking photography courses. We asked them to take pictures for us and they went to La Fontaine Park. So much of our decor came from employees," she tells me.

La Banquise's new owners have said the restaurant likely won't grow beyond its original location. It's unclear how it ever could. Too much of its charm is now baked into its surroundings, with the decades of kitsch as deep as the grease in the deep fryers. As poutine's unassuming main embassy in Montreal, La Banquise has remained relatively small and humble.

"This restaurant is a family to me," Annie says. "It's not just my partner and my sister-in-law working in the office, it's the staff and all the personalities. Without them, there would be no heart to La Banquise. It just wouldn't work. It's more than a potato, some cheese and gravy—it's a story."

So much of that story comes back to the family that nurtured it for decades. The loose atmosphere, the invitation for workers to have fun, the menu run wild with options—all of these were decisions made by someone who wasn't afraid to experiment, while also keeping a booth warm for the late-night regulars. The restaurant somehow packages both discovery and nostalgia into each plate served, helping tourists and new arrivals explore their first poutines while introducing locals to a nearly unconquerable cornucopia of choice.

To keep it going, there's a poutine behemoth behind La Banquise that rivals even Drummondville's busy original. The restaurant's kitchen, staffed by a rotation of over eighty people over the course of each week, uses about 150 kilograms of cheese curds and more than a tonne of red potatoes daily. Unlike other kitchens in this story, there's no break in the schedule for me to go in. Instead, I watch as a constant procession of staff comes out of the kitchen burdened with heavy platters of poutine. The maelstrom inside appears less like a well-oiled machine and more like a ballet, with heapings of fries and various toppings coming together in time for newly returned waiters to turn around and carry away another order that's still steaming.

Annie doesn't see the love for poutine dimming. Quebecers continue to love the dish, she says. "It's a reminder of the province's rural past, those hearty habitants on the land. It's also a comforting meal in difficult times and a supportive one after a night on the town," she says.

Finally, it's time for me to eat. I head over to a table that just freed up. It's bright orange and covered in painted dandelions. Despite the extensive menu in front of me, I've decided to go with a classic. I'd had some time waiting in the snaking line outside the restaurant to chat with first-time tourists to Quebec who had La Banquise on their bucket lists. They told me they wanted to try the classic poutine, to see what all the fuss was about. While I could have gone with a dollop of guacamole or a topping of bacon, I figured it would be best to see what was drawing in the masses—and stick with a choice that would make it easier to compare to the poutines before it on my road trips with my dad.

After a bit of a wait, a poutine was carefully placed in front of me. La Banquise's regular size is a fairly reasonable portion for one person compared to some of the offerings in the province's roadside *casse-croûtes*. The curds are smaller too. Sourced from nearby Fromagerie Champêtre in the Montreal suburb of Repentigny, the cheese is cut into long strips. It's an admittedly odd choice. The fries are freshly out of the deep fryer, dark brown and thick in the style preferred by Quebecers. After my anticipation built as other orders kept going past, my first bite is a release. La Banquise's poutine is a godsend on the Island of Montreal—it's fresh and flavourful, with each of the ingredients packing a hearty punch. While it'll never replace my love for the classics I sampled on the road with my dad, I'm happy to give it two thumbs up.

Sitting in the restaurant, I look at my notes and see how many of Quebec's regions have had a specific role to play in poutine's history. The Centre-du-Québec region, with Warwick and Drummondville, invented the dish. Quebec City with Chez Ashton and lesser-known restaurateurs in places like Trois-Rivières helped spread it across the province. But now, La Banquise has helped serve two further advances.

Later, I ask Annie about the restaurant's impact and she's happy to explain: "We helped bring poutine to Montreal. We didn't invent this wheel, but we're happy that someone did, and then we got to take it, explore it, rediscover it and push it out." The restaurant's other contribution, so clear on the tables around me, was helping push poutine out of its comfort zone and do away with any sense that changing the original recipe would be taboo. It's likely the sheer variety of the offerings in this eclectic restaurant around me would feel like a form of sacrilege if La Banquise hadn't already convinced people otherwise.

And beyond bringing poutine to the metropolis of Montreal, what about its link to the wider world? Did La Banquise help poutine escape Quebec's gravity? I ask Annie. She winces at the question— we're getting close to dangerous ground. "We are so chilly to the idea of taking any credit, but people do tell us that we helped bring poutine to the world," she says, running through the answer quickly, as though she's getting the words out before she regrets them. "People tell us that. We're in a lot of magazines, we're often mentioned. But there are a lot of other restaurants. I'm never going to seize that title or role. I'd be mortified to do it."

Not every restaurant has been recommended by famous American chefs and culinary shows. You get a sense from Annie that as much as the global attention has helped fill all those booths, it also continues to be a distraction on some days, albeit a very small one. "We don't have time to think about that attention. We spend our days ensuring that things go well, that the food is fresh, that the atmosphere is good and that people stay happy," she says.

CHAPTER EIGHT

Taming the
wild West

I WAS PACKING MY BAGS AGAIN A YEAR AFTER THE LAST TRIP DOWN Quebec's poutine highway with my dad. We continued to talk regularly about what we'd seen, and that hour when he practically floated through his old *fromagerie* had stayed with him. He mentioned it often as we continued to try different poutines when we came across them and compared notes. I sampled a few in Ontario, but nothing came close to what I'd had in Quebec.

My time away in "Canada," more precisely downtown Toronto, had been a success professionally and my Canadian adventure was now going to continue in the West with a new job. My first stop was Vancouver, and because a moving budget had been ruled out, I arrived at the airport and life in British Columbia with two checked bags and not the faintest clue what I was doing.

I stayed in Vancouver for a year, sharing a rented attic and surviving on a shoestring budget. But I did eat poutine once. On a rainy day near the end of my time in the city, I ducked into La Belle Patate. With a big Montreal Canadiens flag on the wall and a Pepsi-branded cooler by the counter, I felt like I'd walked into a Quebec diner. After a few words from me, the owner started speaking in French and I forgot where I was in the world. I ordered a poutine and two *steamés*. I gulped down the steamed hot dogs and sized up the poutine. It looked and tasted like many I'd had in Quebec. Before I realized it, I was staring at an empty bowl.

A few weeks later, I was on my way to Edmonton and what would be the beginning of a long stay as a newspaper correspondent in Alberta.

Unlike with that first conversation about moving to Toronto, my dad had been a surprisingly easy sell on Western Canada. I broke the news to him soon after his first—and only—visit to Canada's biggest city. Of course, his visit wasn't exactly by choice. Before the move west, I needed to get an infected wisdom tooth removed and without health insurance, I'd had to shop around—which I would soon discover was not my wisest choice. Once I was in the chair, I found out that the most inexpensive dental surgeon in my area wouldn't use anaesthetic. He would soon be complaining mid-grinding and hammering that the tears streaming down my face were slowing him down.

I woke up the next day with the left side of my face swollen to the size of a grapefruit. My dad offered to come look after me, jumped into his car and drove the seven hours from Trois-Rivières to Toronto.

"You ready to go?" he asks upon walking into my apartment.

"I thought you were going to stay here," I respond through a sore jaw, a little confused.

"*Bin non gars*, let's go to my place," he replies.

"Don't you want to see Toronto? The CN Tower? Any of it?"

"I saw the tower from the highway. Let me use your bathroom and then let's go."

Swollen and in pain, I quickly pack. His total time within Toronto city limits was about forty-five minutes. He's never been back.

Once I can manage solid foods, we naturally head for one of the poutineries closest to his house in Trois-Rivières. A strong smell from the pulp and paper mills hangs in the air—not as pungent as it was when I was young but a constant reminder of the city's history. Our destination is Stratos, which was a favourite of my childhood and has the comfort food I really need. Once we are sitting down in a green leather booth, it's time to tell him I'll be moving even farther away.

"I'm going to Vancouver," I tell him. "To write about the politics and economics of the West."

He nods, not totally surprised. "That sounds nice. I've been to Western Canada. It's nice there. That's where I eventually went after I finished my last milk run and stopped working at the *fromagerie* where I made cheese curds."

He tells me about the night classes he took to learn welding, then the story of how he ended up out west: "On January 4, 1968, I went to the bar to celebrate getting my welding card in the mail. One of my buddies was there and I asked him what he was doing. He said he was leaving the next morning for Manitoba. He was going to build houses in Thompson, this new mining town being built in the far north of the province. There were many jobs then. Entire streets of homes were being built all at once."

Four guys were planning to go—two of them were brothers from his village who he'd known for most of his life, and the third guy owned a Buick that they were going to drive out west. The fourth guy had gone missing. "He'd disappeared into a hotel room earlier that night with a woman and was really drunk. They weren't sure he'd be in condition to go, so they told me, 'We're leaving at nine in the morning. If he's not ready, we're leaving anyway. Why don't you come with us?' I was sitting at the bar and I told them that if he wasn't coming, I was. It was the middle of winter. I didn't have anything else to do anyway."

The Buick rolled into his parents' driveway after breakfast the next morning. The fourth guy had never shown up. My dad's bags were already packed. He said goodbye to my grandfather and headed out the door. "I knew a few English words that I'd learned in school, but none of us had ever left Quebec before. On our first day out there in Canada, we got stopped by a cop in Ontario. I was sitting in the back of the car, but I kind of understood what was happening up front. You have to understand, we were all really drunk. The whole crew. We'd picked up a two-four earlier in the drive and had been passing around beers for hours. The cop kept asking the driver questions and he didn't know a word of English. It was serious, but actually kind of funny." He chuckles at the memory. "I was the only one in the car who had any idea what was going on and I kept quiet. The only words they knew were 'Thompson, Manitoba' and 'Go work.'"

"Did the cops arrest you all?" I ask.

"No," he says. Eventually, the OPP officer got so annoyed that he just told them to go sleep it off in a nearby motel and tailed them to make sure they made it. "The worst of it was that the driver had lost his license a few months back because of drunk driving. You lost it for three months if they caught you drunk behind the wheel. It isn't like today—the system didn't work very well back then."

Three days later the car pulled into Thompson, Manitoba, without further incident. It was mid-January, extremely cold, and my dad quickly discovered he needed a work permit and a construction card. Holding neither, he found a construction foreman, who took him to a nearby shop that needed welders. He was quickly put to work with the only other person who spoke any French.

Without using the words, my dad is painting the scene of an absolutely chaotic boomtown. From there, our conversation quickly descends into the local welding requirements in great detail, going over the different types of flanges, rods and styles of welds the work called for.

As we sit chatting in our booth at Stratos, a waiter comes over with two large regular poutines and two cans of Pepsi. I've been away from Quebec for nearly a year, and I've been thinking about this for a long time. The portions aren't as large as some we had on our road trip, the cheese curds aren't as massive and the fries are a bit greasy, but the aroma transports me back to simpler times. Without prayer or pause, I dig in and close my eyes. Everything about the poutine is slightly imperfect, but it tastes like perfection to a younger part of my mind.

I think about my dad, straight from his small Quebec village, out in Manitoba in the 1960s and unable to speak to the locals beyond a few simple phrases. "Was it hard being a francophone in a place like Thompson in those days?" I ask him.

He shakes his head. "No. We were the only ones, but it wasn't bad," he says. There's a slight pause. "But you know, then I had to come home and take a job in a small welding shop."

I tilt my head in surprise. "If the pay was good, why'd you leave?" I ask him.

"Oh, all the francophones were cleared out over something foolish," he answers.

"Everyone? What was it?" I ask him again.

It quickly becomes clear he isn't trying to hide anything, he just doesn't think it's very important. "We were staying in a work camp outside of Thompson and one of the guys who was with us moonlighted as a taxi driver in town. His name was Jarry and he was a guy from New Brunswick. He spoke perfect English and French—he was pretty much the only person who did. He was a great guy. He knew everyone in town. One night a bunch of English-Canadian guys staying in the camp went into town on a bender. They met some local Indigenous women and brought them back to the work camp. You can't have women in the camp. But they brought them over with promises of beer." He's speaking matter-of-factly, slowly remembering and unspooling events from decades back.

I'm quiet and my heart has sunk into the floorboards. I thought this was going to be a story about discrimination against French

Canadians, but it's taken a much darker turn. He doesn't seem to notice my change of mood and continues.

"Eventually those guys wanted something else. All of a sudden, we're in our room talking and there's some Indigenous women just running down the hallway outside our door and a bunch of these English guys running after them. They notice Jarry in our room—he really knew everyone in town as a taxi driver—and tell him, 'Jarry, these guys are trying to rape us. Help!' Jarry is a big guy, he's six foot three. He went out to talk to the guys. He told them to back off or he was going to call the cops. These women were stuck in the camp, twenty kilometres outside of Thompson. So he drove them back to town. He asked me to come with him. They were in the back and we sat in the front. Nothing happened, we just brought them back to town. But those English guys, they were not happy. They went complaining to the foreman and made up this story that a bunch of Quebec guys had brought these Indigenous women to the camp. It was a pack of lies but they were pissed off at us. The boss came over and fired every single French Canadian on the job. He told us all to pack up and leave immediately. He didn't want to hear a thing. It wasn't our fault, but he let us all go." He takes a bite of poutine as he finishes. There's still a hint of frustration in his voice.

I'm astonished. I'll think back on this story, this one snippet of life in a single camp on a single day, while reporting later on the National Inquiry into Missing and Murdered Indigenous Women and Girls and the testimony that survivors shared from decades of violence.

"So when I asked you if there were problems…" I look at my dad, not sure what to say. It seems like being framed and told to leave on a moment's notice without the possibility of defending yourself would count as a problem.

"Like that? Sure, okay, there were a lot of problems," he concedes. He explains that they befriended a Franco-Ontarian woman in town, the wife of one of the workers, and she went to the bank with them when they cashed their paycheques. The French workers had figured out the cashiers were skimming too much off, and the banks were charging too many fees. They might not have known the language, but they could do math. "It wasn't always super easy," he adds. Our poutines are both almost finished and while they are tasty, I can't really think about the taste.

He would spend most of the next decade on the road, often closer to home, but interspersed with long periods of time spent around the country. He helped build a refinery outside Edmonton, a city he remembers fondly. He built ships near Quebec City—"a really dangerous and dirty business"—and welded in a soaring chemical complex in Sarnia, Ontario. He got to see much of Canada and developed an appreciation for the country that lasts to this day. He became a skilled welder and, during a job in Cape Breton, got taken on as an inspector. The new position paid more, was less physically demanding and held the promise of a different career trajectory—toward something that was more manager and less grunt.

He was hired to be an inspector on the construction of the Point Lepreau nuclear power station in New Brunswick. It was a big deal: he'd sign off on the welds holding together a nuclear plant. "I did that for two years. I was a white hat, the one little Québécois amid thousands of English-Canadian guys. It was demanding work, and we'd catch some guys cutting corners, not doing the welds right and trying to hide it. Sometimes I'd reject someone's work and later I'd go in the bathroom and see that they'd written 'Frenchie' with an unfriendly qualifier after it. People would point fingers at me. It wasn't very fun, but it was my job. When it was done, the company wanted to send me to Sherbrooke and put me in charge of an entire work site. They already had another job in Ontario lined up for me after that."

"But you didn't do that," I say.

"I said no. I went back to my union local and hung my chit on the board to work as a welder again. I didn't want to be a boss. It was never in my nature to be a boss, to give orders. I felt more like a man when I worked, did the job, even if it was harder." He would remain a welder for the rest of his working life, only stopping in his seventies when his knees and back started giving out.

I remind him again of what he'd said earlier, that he'd had no issue being a French Canadian while out in English Canada. "I meant I didn't have any trouble figuring things out, what I needed to do. I get along with most people. I just like to laugh and things go well," he says. He's never given the more troublesome side of things much thought. Before this conversation, he's never mentioned facing discrimination and hasn't displayed any sign of grievance—and he won't mention it ever again after the conversation either. Instead, he turns back toward the positive. He worked hard and got to see cities he'd only read about in schoolbooks or heard about on the news. He also pocketed money along the way, then bought a nice convertible, raced it around a track near his hometown with his friends and ate his first poutine.

As we finished our lunch, it was nearing time for me to wish my dad another goodbye. This one would be more lasting, with no promise of a great bonding road trip in our future. He gave me a pat on the back and there was a tear in his eye as I boarded a bus back to Toronto later that afternoon.

It was time to head west. I put most of what I owned in a Toronto storage locker and took the rest of my belongings in two bags to the airport. I thought about what my father had told me, not so much begrudgingly revealing secrets as accidentally opening floodgates without realizing what would come through. Before the start of our poutine journey, he hadn't spoken much about his past, not out of shame or reservation, but because he didn't think anyone would care.

Poutine had helped open him up a bit. I was now getting a peek, one that helped me better understand my father and a struggle he'd never shared before. The anti-"Frenchie" bathroom graffiti had turned history into something tangible.

I spoke with him over the phone while I was in Vancouver. Conversation came more easily than before, but my French grew rustier the longer I was away. I spent more time searching for my words. After a year away from Quebec, I packed my two bags again and landed in Alberta, not quite sure what I'd find.

I arrived in Edmonton a few weeks before Christmas in the middle of a snowstorm. My first day in the city was lost in the basement of the provincial legislature, looking for my new office. It turned out to be an oversized mop closet that would become my real home for the next three years. About a minute after I sat down, a senior government official poked her head into the open door: "You're the new guy? From Quebec? Welcome. We don't care about that language crap here, but Alberta loves people who work hard," she told me, her tone happy. She then offered to help outfit my new apartment with the unused contents of her daughter's hope chest.

I hadn't been looking for poutine in Alberta, but a few weeks after my arrival I stumbled into it unexpectedly. On a trip to Calgary, in the shade of tall office towers bearing the names of large oil companies, I found myself at a tavern flipping through the menu. To my surprise, the poutine selection would have fit in at any restaurant in rural Quebec—with one very large exception. This bar, having shared the realization of many that poutine is a dish best shared, had created a monster size that would leave any Quebecer blushing. Their largest poutine, advertised prominently on the menu, was served in a punchbowl and came with half a kilo of cheese curds, two kilos of fries and a litre of gravy. I wasn't up to eating a bowling ball's worth of poutine—in weight—but I was impressed.

Throughout Alberta, I found poutines on restaurant menus every-where, served as everything from breakfast to midnight snacks. There was also a wave of new poutine-only restaurants opening, includ-ing ones with surprisingly fresh curds in downtown Edmonton and Calgary. I'd seen poutine on some menus in Toronto and Vancouver, but it was nearly ubiquitous in Calgary. The city's poutine selection was intense. When I asked around about where this poutine ren-aissance had come from, one name kept coming up: Karen Richards.

I meet Richards at a small coffee shop in Calgary's trendy Beltline neighbourhood. She's wearing a jean jacket and her brown hair is spill-ing over her shoulders. There is unfortunately no poutine on the menu at the java joint. Energetic and happy to talk about poutine, she quickly gets to explaining how she's ridden Calgary's poutine wave and may have helped it out along the way. It started in 2009 when Richards was searching for a social media topic to bring to a public relations class she was teaching at Calgary's Mount Royal University. Her goal was to prove that anyone could build a strong social media strategy around something simple.

"It came down to bacon or poutine. They both were something that people spoke a lot about, so I asked them questions, like how often they eat poutine, how they feel about traditional versus unusual, the trifecta of ingredients and which is the most important. I was trying to see what conversation would get going, and poutine was hands-down the winner," Richards tells me. Our coffees arrive, cappuccinos with an inch of foam on top and thick with chocolate shavings.

A very unscientific poll of students and Twitter turned into Poutine with Purpose, a Calgary-wide poutine crawl that has now gone on for more than a decade. As much as it's a celebration of pou-tine, there's a strong charity aspect. For each poutine sold during the festival, money is donated to provide a meal to someone in need.

The interest in poutine was already bubbling in Calgary when Richards got the ball rolling. While she's turned into a poutine expert now, she had no real background in cooking, the dish itself or Quebec when she started. She's never been to Drummondville. She doesn't speak French. "And at the very beginning I thought it was from Montreal," she says with a look of pain.

"I grew up in Calgary, and poutine wasn't a thing in the eighties or nineties. It's a Canadian classic and everyone loves it now. But there's still a debate every year with people from Montreal who have moved to Calgary and argue that it isn't real poutine here," she tells me.

"What is it that sets them off?" I ask her.

"Oh, it's the curds."

Around 2009, poutine was still a novelty in Calgary. The first local restaurant with a poutine-specific menu had only emerged a few years before I arrived, Richards tells me now, years after the poutine festival got underway. She then launches into a story to illustrate her point: "My sister had gone to Montreal after we got started, and I told her she had to try the poutine. I gave her a list of places to go. She came back and told me it was amazing. Guess where she went? A&W. I was so disappointed."

Despite her lack of deep poutine knowledge at the start, she stuck with the idea and took it to her class, told them what she planned to do and explained that it wouldn't be an easy project. She billed it as a fun experiment in word-of-mouth marketing. Things started small. She brushed up on poutine and learned "why the cheese needs to squeak. That's important," she remembers.

That first year she launched with a single-day affair. Using only Twitter, she convinced eighty people to pay up front for a bus that would shuttle them between six restaurants that had put together unusual poutines. "We did it like that for three years. It was so successful. It was great for the course because eating poutine is really a fun topic," she tells me.

Putting down her coffee, Richards takes a moment to pull out a poutine-flavoured lip balm she got from La Poutine, a food truck in Edmonton. "It's a good lip balm, but it creates quite a reaction," she says. I give it a try. It smells like cheese. And it kind of tastes like cheese on the lips. I can see how it could be a conversation starter, but I'm also struck that an Albertan business has gone to the trouble of creating a poutine-flavoured lip balm as a marketing gimmick.

From that one bus full of poutine aficionados, Poutine with Purpose has grown into a passion project for Richards. Running a full week, it now includes over one hundred restaurants. One thing that sets this festival apart is the absolute rainbow of flavours the restaurants create.

The creativity was there right at the beginning. During the first poutine crawl, chef Roy Oh created a Korean poutine at his Anju restaurant. A place called La Brasserie created a foie gras poutine that was "really decadent, yet still French," Richards remembers. Another restaurant, National, had a modern take that used Japanese-style miso vegetarian gravy.

"The chefs love it because it brings new customers in, and they want the challenge of making something different. We have sushi restaurants creating poutine with yam fries. They get really creative," she says. The one thing that isn't on the menu in most of the restaurants involved is the traditional dish. Despite all the poutines I've sampled in Calgary, many of the places that sign up for the festival don't make poutine outside of that one week.

Richards hands me her phone and shows me the plan for the next edition of the festival. The café is loud and we're leaning in close to talk. The list of poutines is eye-popping, with a vast assortment of ingredients and cuisines involved. There are poutines based on tacos, perogies, cheeseburgers, lamb vindaloo, mille feuilles, cottage pies, Korean chicken, brioche, donairs, nachos, gyros, banh mi sandwiches and several different hot sauces. One memorable poutine is called a Ricky Bobby, based on the Will Ferrell character from the movie *Talladega Nights*, which incorporates Shake 'n Bake. This absolutely unexpected appearance seems in the spirit of the Elvis poutine at La Banquise in Montreal. Overall, this varied selection would make even the most vocal supporter of La Banquise's many options go wide-eyed.

The festival's focus has broadened in recent years. A professional extreme eater joined the event a few years back. He'd given himself the challenge of eating all fifty poutines at that year's festival in one week. He tapped out after thirty-six. No one else has taken up the challenge.

There's also been talk about bringing cannabis into the mix. The event is held every April and there could be a competition on 4/20 for chefs to include edibles in their poutines. Richards is looking forward to little edibles shaped like cheese curds. It certainly would cut out the middleman when it comes to poutine and the munchies.

That specific idea has been picked up in Quebec by the government-owned cannabis retailer, the SQDC, which now sells a poutine gravy infused with THC.

The festival hasn't been completely positive for Richards. Her attempts to reach out to organizers of other festivals in Quebec have yielded nothing good. She has only heard a reply in the form of legal pushback. As poutine has turned into big business, the lawyers have become involved. Poutine with Purpose was initially known as Poutine Week. A Montreal-based company trademarked the words Poutine Week after she'd started her festival and hit her with a cease and desist. She tried to explain that she was running a non-profit that turns over any proceeds to charity. No luck, so the festival became Poutine with Purpose. "We didn't think they were being very neighbourly. I can't quite believe they actually paid money to trademark the term and then send me a legal letter," she says.

While the legal threat made no mention of it, Richards understands there's some tension around how poutine is labelled. While her default is to call poutine Canadian, she concedes that Quebec's clear attachment should be respected. But few locals would understand, she adds.

"Western Canadians feel like it's a Canadian thing. As Canadians, we all get to say that it's ours, that's the feeling. I tell people, Caesars and poutine, that's ours. It's like Tim Hortons coffee, but in a good way," she says with an expansive shrug. "What would Quebec traditionalists think if they took a trip to Calgary for our poutine? Would they be mortified or proud?"

Calgary's poutine scene wouldn't exist without its chefs. One of the driving forces behind Poutine with Purpose since the beginning has been Roy Oh. His culinary approach to poutine is about as far from rural Quebec as could be imagined. Born and raised in Edmonton, he has an appreciation of where poutine started and what makes one truly good, but he's not at all interested in trying to reproduce a classic poutine on the Prairies. Instead, he wants to make it like Korean street food.

"I like to eat the traditional poutine, but for the festival, it's fun to figure out a different way to present poutine with Korean flair, because that's what we do," he tells me. We've met in a bar near downtown Calgary hidden inside what looks like a regular house. We retreat to a dark corner and start talking about cheese curds.

The first poutine Oh ever made was for the festival's first year. He'd never made one professionally or at home before. "It was so weird. We didn't even use potatoes anywhere on our menu, so I just fried up rice sticks and then, obviously, added cheese curds and spicy Asian-style gravy," he explains.

The poutine was a hit inside the kitchen. So he created a competition before the next year's event, telling his cooks to come up with the best poutine they could. After a taste-off in the kitchen, the winner would be added to the restaurant's menu for the festival. "It obviously had to be Korean-inspired, but it also needed to taste good. It's all about the flavour. There's temperature and texture—all those factors make something delicious. With poutine, you can't use soggy fries. You need them to be crunchy so when you pour gravy on them, they stay crispy," he says. It is an animated discussion of food, and our two beers make circles through the air as we talk.

He's coming to the latest edition of the festival with a corn cheese poutine that has waffle fries, cheese curds, corn, mozzarella sauce, an egg and nori. It's not clear yet what the judges will think. "There's just such a great range of poutine at the festival. Some people go pretty traditional and just elevate it a bit. That's nice. But sometimes you get things like a carbonara poutine or something just completely different," he says excitedly. "One year I made one like Korean curry with tater tots—that was pretty messed up!"

Originality and culinary experimentation aren't a problem for the festival. Instead, the greatest challenge Oh faces is the same as nearly every other purveyor of poutine: buying fresh curds in Alberta is, at the time of writing, just about impossible. Some artisanal operations turn them out in small batches, but the taste and market just aren't there. "We ordered our curds through our GFS supplier. Then Karen got us a supply of cheese curds from somewhere more local, a brand called Squeakers or something. I'm not sure where, but it was a much higher-quality product," he explains.

GFS, or Gordon Food Service, is one of the largest food distributors in North America. If you've eaten out this week, you've likely eaten something supplied by GFS. As might be expected from a giant with supply chains that cross the world, GFS's cheese curds don't quite meet Quebec's standards. They're listed by the company as twenty-nine per cent milk fat, which is a little low, but also as "individually quick frozen." You work with what you've got. The better curds, as Oh describes them, aren't strictly local. They're from Winnipeg. Fromagerie Bothwell in Manitoba's largest city turns out a few different types of cheese curds under its Squeak'rs brand. If you find yourself in Western Canada, you might come across them in the cooler at a local supermarket. While they've been refrigerated, "they still have some squeak," Oh assures me.

So why does this noisiest of cheeses squeak? At a microscopic level, cheese curds are a tough web of protein fibres held together by calcium. When you bite into them, the protein and calcium rub against your teeth, making a squeaky protest as you break them apart. After a day or two, the calcium dissolves and the protein grows soft. Instead of that tough structure that squeaks between your chompers, the curd starts deflating and its musical properties come to an end.

When they're good, cheese curds squeak loudly between your teeth—which explains why Bothwell would have chosen the name Squeak'rs. A popular brand in Quebec even goes by the tagline of "Skouik! Skouik!"—capturing its full onomatopoeic value. Eating a handful of them can sound like a basketball team scuffing up a freshly waxed court.

Keeping that squeak is a challenge and remains one of the main brakes on poutine's spread. The easiest solution is to make it locally and eat it fresh. However, even in Calgary, a city with significant demand for poutine and the wealth to pay for it, the logistics of cheese curd production just aren't around in any significant volume. Instead, one of the simplest cheeses, cheddar-based curds, are trucked hundreds, sometimes thousands of kilometres to the city and across Canada in refrigerated trailers. However, there is research underway to find whether there are ways to prolong the squeak.

I reached Arthur Hill for guidance on what's happening in the cheese world. A professor at the University of Guelph and cheese expert who came recommended by his peers as the best curd guy around, Hill is now retired and spends most of his spare time with his grandchildren. But he found a few minutes to chat cheese. He'll be the first to admit there isn't a lot of research underway in Canada on the humble curd. But the final piece of research he supervised before his retirement was a challenge of whether the twenty-four-hour rule for safely keeping curds at room temperature is still fit for purpose.

To do so, he made a batch of curds you really wouldn't want to eat. "Essentially, we took the two most common pathogens and inoculated cheese curds with those," he tells me. Specifically, the pathogens were listeria and staphylococcus aureus. Most people know listeria from product recalls; it's a bacteria that causes mild to severe food poisoning. Staphylococcus aureus on the other hand is one of the world's leading causes of antimicrobial resistance and has a nasty rap sheet. You don't want to eat it if you can avoid it.

Hill continues, a bit cheerfully: "So we made cheese curds in our pilot plant at the university, took samples of cheese we made to the lab, and we inoculated them with one or the other and watched to see what would grow." He clarifies that they couldn't bring the pathogens to a plant that makes cheese that people then study and eat because that really wouldn't be a good idea.

So what did they learn? "We went so far as to test for forty-eight hours. Both of the organisms did not grow, which is a good result, but we couldn't really recommend keeping it out beyond that period of time," he tells me. The concern is that when someone buys cheese curds within twenty-four hours of manufacture, as legally required, they might not eat them within that twenty-four-hour window. At a gas station, during an impulse buy, the curds will likely be eaten quickly. However, a larger bag from the grocery store might sit around for another day at home. According to their findings, you'll likely be fine if that happens.

Forty-eight hours isn't enough time to get fresh cheese curds across the country and isn't legal under Canada's food rules either. Hill confirms that yes, the best, squeakiest cheese curd is fresh, right out of the vat. But he offers a surprising follow-up: "If you want to maintain the curd with the most squeak possible, you'll actually cool it immediately after it's made. That way, when it's rewarmed, you'll get a better squeak than if you'd waited to cool it."

The primary structural unit of a cheese curd is the protein casein. Fat and salt are also important, but casein is key. It holds everything together and, when the acidity is just right, casein squeaks when you break it apart. Caseins are hydrophobic, which means they don't like water. When they are fresh or warm, casein particles are drawn to each other and aren't water-soluble—which is also why they don't melt quickly under hot gravy. As a curd ages, its acidity increases and the caseins stop pulling together as tightly, meaning the structure of the curd loosens, it stops being as chewy and the squeak goes away. The sweet spot for temperature is room temperature.

Hill has done the research to show that the aging of a curd, to a point, can be thrown in reverse with a little heat. "Take it from the fridge to the microwave and it's fine. In fact, I've told many people that. You don't want to overdo it and get it too hot—then it'll melt and fuse and leave you with a completely different product. As long as it's heated uniformly and you don't go beyond thirty degrees Celsius, it will squeak," he says. The higher temperature from a few seconds of microwaving means those casein particles and the structure of curds, with their squeak, will bounce back.

I tried it out at home and it does work. A limp, cold curd that spent the night in the refrigerator was squeaky and chewy again after four seconds of microwave time—don't wait too long. For refrigeration and heating to work best, the cheese needs to be cooled as early as possible, before the acid has started eating away at the inside of the cheese. The acid's destructive process can't be reversed. However, for poutine restaurants outside of Quebec, this fast cooling and warming strategy could be the difference between bad curds and something that tastes like it just came out of the factory. Just add a little heat.

I share some of this intel with Roy Oh. The ability to improve on what's available for cheese curds bodes well for poutine's future in the West—and Calgary chefs, like chefs everywhere, love eating poutine on their own time. "If I go out, I'll choose the most traditional one, or sometimes I'll get some Montreal smoked meat on top," Oh says. "The popularity of poutine is because it's something that's, well, perfect. That's why it's become what it is today. When you start messing with it, you can be creative and try things, but don't mess with the base. I only do the creative poutines for fun at work," he says.

Throughout my conversations with Richards and Oh, both have been very careful when speaking about poutine's identity. There's a bubbling undercurrent that English Canada has either taken or borrowed Quebec's poutine. Oh tells me he doesn't really worry much about the wider conversation. "In the culinary world, there's always people pushing to create new things from old things. That's exciting. If I'm making a Korean-style poutine and people are enjoying it, I don't see how anyone could have a problem with that," he says. He takes a moment to sip his beer. "I guess if I was a Quebecer, I could see how that feeling might exist: that now it's becoming Canada's food and is losing its identity. I could see that. But people I know from Quebec are really proud of poutine, and they've got a lot to be proud of."

I bring up Karen Richards's earlier question about how those Quebecers sitting at the Roy Jucep in Drummondville might react to the wild poutines Oh and other chefs have planned. "Oh, I think they'd be mortified." But as much as Poutine with Purpose is about fun and games between chefs, it also has a serious mission to raise money to feed the needy. As much as he loves the fun, that's the reason Oh wants more chefs to join the festival. "If I have to make up a weird, messed-up poutine to help feed some kids, I'll do it," he says.

From sea to sea to sea?

A S POUTINE HAS UNDERGONE A RAPID BURST OF CULINARY expansion in recent decades, becoming a Canada-wide food, one thing has remained unchanged. Whether it's dished up at a roadside *casse-croûte* or served on a white tablecloth in a temple of fine dining, Quebecers continue to feel a deep attachment to their poutine.

It's Quebec's poutine and Quebec's dish, as I was often reminded during my travels through the province with my dad. Restaurants in Toronto and Edmonton make it with cheddar and other oddities, Quebecers would tell me time and time again when asked about "Canadian" poutine. Other Canadians don't know poutine, and if they do, they can't make it very well. There's a certainty to those feelings. However, under the bravado and protestations from Drummondville to Quebec City about the province's poutine superiority, there also seems to lie a real fear. Is it possible that a uniquely Québécois symbol— one that has helped define so many small towns and given so many patrons a powerful reminder of home—might also be slipping away?

Stuck in the middle, I soon learned, is La Banquise. As a popular destination for tourists, it maintains a website that has to balance the emotions brought on by the changing nature of poutine's identity. The restaurant provides a history of poutine in both English and French.

Both versions describe poutine as "our national dish." It's a subtle and cunning way to sidestep a debate that has been brewing, very gently, on the back burner.

On occasion, the debate and feared loss of a national symbol has boiled over onto the front pages of Quebec's more populist tabloids. So how has La Banquise managed? A Quebecer reading that line from the website would likely nod to what's clearly a reference to poutine's importance to the nation of Quebec. An English Canadian, reading the same words in English, would likely come to the conclusion that it actually refers to Canada's national dish. That's the essence of a debate that is not likely to go away soon: is poutine Québécois? Is it Canadian? Can it be both?

As a child of both worlds, I thought back to that first conversation with my dad at the kitchen table in my apartment, and his worry that my imminent move to English Canada would mean a loss for him and, in a very small way, the Quebec nation.

To get a sense of how she managed, I called up Annie Barsalou with more questions. She quickly confirmed that she often finds herself on the frontlines of the identity conflict behind the counter at La Banquise. "For a tourist coming from Japan or Europe, everything in Canada is Canada. We're not Quebec. For them, it's all Canada. We tell them that poutine, yes, it's from Canada, but the source is Quebec. We try to present it that way," Barsalou explains. The balancing act doesn't always work. Almost daily a patron will ask for Barsalou or a member of her staff to take a stronger stand on Quebec's rights to the dish. She finds the topic's longevity both exasperating and bewildering, frankly.

"Someone complained recently to me from Western Canada. They took the time to write an email and demanded I stop calling it Canadian." She takes a moment to laugh at the absurdity of someone in the West trying to lecture a Quebecer who has sold poutine for decades. "I try to explain to them that Quebec is part of Canada. I write that when I'm speaking to someone from overseas, I tell them it's Québécois-Canadian from Drummondville. The story we tell people really depends on where you're from and what you understand. There's no reason to get angry over this. I find it unfortunate when people fight about poutine."

Nicolas Fabien-Ouellet didn't mean to start a fight when he published a paper titled "Poutine Dynamics" in the academic journal *Cuizine: The Journal of Canadian Food Cultures* a few days before Christmas in 2016. At most, his goal was to tap the brakes on poutine's spreading identity and start an academic discussion about what he saw as the growing "Canadianizing" of poutine. But mostly, he just wanted to write about something he loves as part of his master's degree.

His paper hit Quebec's media like an artillery shell. At one end of a suddenly expanding debate, the newspaper *La Presse* interviewed English-speaking culinary experts who lambasted the growing debate over poutine's identity as a ridiculous fabrication designed to drive attention. There was some concession to the clear echoes of the debate over Quebec's place in Canada that had reverberated in that newspaper's editorial pages for decades, but it was quickly brushed aside as a little too absurd. At the other end of the reaction spectrum, the *Journal de Montreal*'s enormous readership was exposed to what its columnists described as another sad tale of cultural appropriation of a beloved Quebec symbol by hungry English Canadians. The provincial motto of *"Je me souviens"* was invoked, adding poutine's capture by English Canada as another entry in the long ledger of glories and misfortunes since the creation and fall of New France centuries earlier.

The timing couldn't have been better for Fabien-Ouellet. Poutine had been on the menu at the White House a few months earlier when Canadian Prime Minister Justin Trudeau and US president Barack Obama met for the first time. The once rural dish had been transformed into a canapé by White House executive chef Cristeta Comerford—and it was nothing like a classic poutine from Drummondville. Her take featured shavings of smoked duck on cheese curds, along with red wine gravy, all placed on a bed of delicate wafer fries. This set up the main course, which was a far more pedestrian lamb with potato. Poutine was now officially at the pinnacle of fine dining.

Those culinary choices and the sight of a "poutine" in the White House were reverberating as Fabien-Ouellet got writing. A master's student from Quebec studying food systems at the University of Vermont, he was drawn to the elevation of a dish that had been long stigmatized as a symbol of Quebec backwardness to a state dinner hosted by a US president. His internal radar told him something was happening with the status of poutine.

Years after his paper first appeared, I sit down with Fabien-Ouellet at Patati Patata, a small poutine-focused restaurant near Montreal's bustling Marché Jean-Talon. It was my first time at this outpost of Patati, but I'd spent many nights at the original location, a bohemian diner on Saint-Laurent Boulevard that squeezes a dozen people into a space not much larger than a parking spot. Fabien-Ouellet, in his early thirties, is neatly dressed and flashes a boyish grin as he finds his chair.

He's now the director general of the city's large system of public food markets and spends his days worrying about deliveries of fruits and vegetables. But for the next hour, he's forgotten all about that as we begin talking about one of his oldest passions. "I really hadn't set out to write about poutine," he tells me. He had his eyes set on more exotic fare, but soon after he arrived in Vermont, his thesis supervisor led him to the idea.

"I was going to study the interaction of culture, people and their food. When I arrived, my supervisor quickly told me, 'You're not from here. You're from two hours away, but it's a whole different culture, identity and foods up there. Tell us more about that great Canadian dish that is poutine.' When they told me that, I don't know why, but it sounded off to my ears," he says, pausing to ponder what came next.

"The word *Canadian*," he explains. "It landed with a blow. So I started looking into it and quickly saw that there was evidence of poutine being slowly recategorized as more than just Québécois, as something bicultural and more broadly Canadian. I thought then, 'Is it being taken, appropriated?'" The question stuck.

"I told my thesis supervisor that I might have something on poutine for a paper. I took two months off in the summer for research and promised to come back and show what I had. Then I thought about my own relationship with poutine. That was the spark," he says.

Originally from Montreal, Fabien-Ouellet grew up in Quebec City. His youth was one marked by the emergence of poutine. He's a fellow millennial, of a generation younger than my dad and unable to remember his first poutine. "It was nearly always there," he remembers. A turbulent point during his adolescence was when his high school principal ordered poutine withdrawn from the cafeteria menu. The move was part of a health wave in the province, and poutine was henceforth limited to Thursdays, giving rise in Fabien-Ouellet's school to a cottage industry devoted to getting students to the front of the weekly poutine line. He smiles as he remembers how pushing, running and dirty tricks so you wouldn't miss the limited poutine supply became the norm. That ended when students discovered that a neighbouring ice rink had added poutine to its canteen menu. The cafeteria quickly emptied out as word spread that the arena's poutine was also far superior to the high school's fare.

Poutine wasn't really on Fabien-Ouellet's mind after high school as something contentious or worth debating. It was just there. As he turned his thoughts toward poutine during his university research trip, he quickly found a food unlike any other in Quebec.

"No other food screams more Québécois than poutine," he told me. Sure, the province has other foods it loves, like *bouilli* (a beef ragout often served around Christmas), *pâté chinois* (shepherd's pie), sugar pies and all the other dishes that come out over the holidays in homes across the province. But there's an important difference: those foods are mostly enjoyed in private residences, cooked up in home kitchens for friends and family. "That makes those dishes hard to share," he explains. "However, with poutine, when you visit Quebec you can have it everywhere, and that's how you discover Quebec, that's how you taste it. Even if you don't speak French, you can have a taste of Quebec through poutine."

As Fabien-Ouellet speaks, two plates of classic poutine are put down in front of us. An important thing to understand, he says, is that poutine is a social dish. Whether you are stopping at a roadside *casse-croûte* or wrapping up a night out, poutine is often meant to be eaten with others. Not just in terms of having individual portions for a number of people, but in the act of actually sharing a single plate. "People often buy the largest size they can and get a few forks to share," he says. I nod, realizing I'd done this only days earlier with a group of friends. While my dad isn't here, I've adopted his role of nodding along and encouraging.

"What other dish do you share so readily?" he asks me.

The cheese and fries make it easy. Sharing also helps make the poutine itself the topic of discussion. People can talk about how fresh the cheese is and whether they like the gravy. And Quebecers do love debating poutine. I'm part of a few active groups on social media that debate the merits of different poutines found across Quebec in minute detail. It's honest, sometimes harsh, but never mean. I mention this to Fabien-Ouellet and he immediately agrees. "I'm on some of those groups too."

The main reaction to his paper was a political debate about poutine's status. Forget for a moment the larger question of Quebec within Canada and focus on poutine itself, a simple dish with three ingredients. Poutine's reputation has shifted sharply over the past half century. "It's one of those foods that has gone from shame to delicacy," Fabien-Ouellet says.

Neither of us have touched our poutines in the few minutes since a waiter brought them over. We're sitting near the back of the restaurant, and there are few diners nearby to notice the two guys largely oblivious to the world around them, deep in debate. The restaurant is dark and modern. I take out a red pen and start writing notes on my paper placemat. Fabien-Ouellet doesn't miss a beat as he explains his thesis.

"I looked at this hierarchy of taste. Poutine is the same as it was fifty years ago, but the perception of the group eating it has completely changed. Where it was once mocked, poutine is now praised, and that reflects a new praise for Québécois culture. The same thing happened with sushi. During World War II, the Japanese were treated with suspicion—and in America, as a group, they were jailed for it. Their food was seen as backward. Eating raw fish was considered dangerous and disgusting. Today it's seen as one of the world's highest-end dishes—people pay a lot to eat raw fish when it's in sushi. That reflects an incredible change in the cultural capital of that group, one from a 'backward people' who eat raw food to a prestigious global economic power."

Similarly, families in the Maritimes once tried to keep their lobster-eating ways under wraps, so as not to be seen eating what was best reserved for lunatics or fertilizer. Even Italian cuisine was seen as backward a century ago, with those raised with more British palates aghast at all the pasta and garlic.

After tracing poutine's rise from mockery to acceptance, Fabien-Ouellet's most contentious and difficult conclusion is this: poutine can't be seen as both Québécois and Canadian. "How could something with such a history of being used as a means of bringing shame and mockery to Quebec by other Canadians be considered Canadian?" he muses. He doesn't even see this as something all that worthy of debate anymore. It's so obvious where poutine's identity is and where it should remain. Around us, the restaurant has nearly emptied out. Our poutines are still warm, but the steam has stopped coming off them.

"It's well understood in Quebec that there is a distinction between cultures. There's a Quebec literature, a Quebec film industry and a Quebec cuisine. It's not the same thing as elsewhere. Saying that poutine is Canadian is the same as saying that Québécois literature is Canadian and that Quebec films are Canadian too. If that's true, what does it mean for other groups in Canada? Are First Nations, Metis and Inuit people all part of the same Canadian group as well? Obviously not," he says.

He picks up his fork and starts scooping up his poutine. "This is a good poutine," he says between bites. I push aside the restaurant's trademark olive, sitting on the little mound of cheese on top of my poutine, and try for myself. The instantly recognizable taste of a Patati Patata poutine hits—the restaurant uses thinner fries and its gravy isn't as rich as some others, but there's a reason it's been a Montreal favourite for years.

Fabien-Ouellet picks back up the conversation. "The conclusion here isn't that we need to stick with what made a classic Québécois poutine forever. Cultures need to balance control and growth, but they need to evolve," he says. The process is already underway, with vegan cheese curds and exotic meats from around the world being added to poutine in recent years.

Some of poutine's ongoing cultural adaption is visible in Montreal's vibrant Haitian community. A number of restaurants around the city now serve poutine with *griot*, a traditional Haitian dish of pork shoulder marinated in citrus, then braised and fried. "It wouldn't be fair to say that a *griot* poutine isn't poutine because it doesn't just have the three classic ingredients. That's a poutine that's now unique to Montreal. You can't find it in Haiti, only here. This is a culture that's growing," says Fabien-Ouellet.

I wasn't quite satisfied leaving it there. To get another point of view on the debate, I meet with Ian Cuthbertson. He's a teacher at Montreal's Dawson College, a part of the provincial CEGEP system that students need to attend between high school and university. As a post-doctoral fellow at Queen's University in Ontario, Cuthbertson ended up looking at poutine as part of his research into how beliefs and behaviours become religions. There's no poutine religion, of course (at least not yet). Like Fabien-Ouellet before him, he got interested in what he perceived as the rapidly changing cultural views around poutine. He came to the opposite conclusion.

We chose to meet at the Greenspot restaurant in Montreal's francophone Saint-Henri neighbourhood. The place has served poutine for decades and is close to the wealthy English enclave of Westmount, straddling the city's linguistic divide.

Writing about poutine's identity in a 2017 peer-reviewed blog post entitled "Politicizing Poutine," Cuthbertson concluded that the whole debate about whether poutine is Canadian or Québécois was deeply political, with both sides attempting to construct an identity that served its own interests. Poutine is both Canadian and Québécois, he wrote at the time.

His is an interesting counterpoint to Fabien-Ouellet's background. Cuthbertson is an anglophone Quebecer from Montreal's English-speaking West Island, but he's still a Quebecer and deeply invested in the idea of poutine.

"Has your view that poutine hasn't been appropriated by English Canadians softened at all in recent years as the dish's popularity has grown outside Quebec?" I ask him at the start of a discussion that will go on for over an hour.

"It has not," he tells me. He has large, stylish glasses and a shaved head, along with a five o'clock shadow. He isn't teaching today, so he's wearing a more casual shirt.

"I don't know if anyone in Quebec is really worried about the cultural appropriation of poutine now that it is everywhere in the country. It isn't a big social question. There are enough burning social questions in Quebec," he continues. "But that doesn't mean we can't talk about poutine's identity."

Like Fabien-Ouellet, he's concerned about the history of the dish. As an anglophone academic, he doesn't pull any punches about how his own historic community—and half of my heritage as well—has treated the dish we're now preparing to order at the Greenspot. Our conversation is in English, while everything around us in the restaurant is being conducted in French. "Poutine was just a stand-in, yet another way for anglophone Quebecers to differentiate themselves from francophone Quebecers. For the rest of the country, it was that classic 'two solitudes' thing—but with gravy. It added to this notion that Quebec is separate, different and odd," says Cuthbertson.

His moment of interest in poutine didn't come from a thesis supervisor—it came from anger. After McDonald's, Burger King, Harvey's, KFC and A&W added poutine to their Canadian menus during the 2000s, the American-owned Wendy's burger chain decided to join the crowded pack in 2012. To make a splash with its new menu item, the company launched a large advertising campaign to have poutine crowned as "Canada's national dish." The campaign went absolutely nowhere, and Quebec was largely left out of it. While Cuthbertson has dismissed the cries of cultural appropriation, he was offended by an American company's campaign to officially have poutine declared Canadian. The more he thought about it, the madder he got.

"It feels odd, but it fires me up. My mother is Italian, my father is Irish, and I'm Montreal-born. Insofar as I have a culture, it's this one. Then Wendy's comes along. Who do they think they are? Wendy's! Wendy's? An American burger joint trying to claim a Quebec dish as Canada's dish to sell what's really just their inferior poutine." He's still feeling the outrage a decade later.

As he sees it, claiming poutine as a national dish for Canada is nonsensical. "It doesn't exist from coast to coast. It seemed like just another thing that Canada was taking that was quintessentially Quebec and trying to establish it as a marker of Canadian identity. The idea of appropriation—even though I disagreed with it—was interesting to me because Quebec does not need to go searching for markers of national identity. The markers are plentiful and obvious—language is just one of them. However, the rest of the country does need to go searching for markers of Canadian cultural identity. I just don't know what those should be. If you define a marker as something that exists and is shared from coast to coast to coast, there's pretty much nothing. Even things like maple syrup, poutine, toques and ice hockey. That's all very Quebec!" he declares with real feeling.

Despite the efforts of governments and businesses to create a pan-Canadian identity out of Tim Hortons cups and concepts like multiculturalism, others have also rejected the idea. Justin Trudeau said during his early days as prime minister that Canada is a country that shouldn't have a core identity, leading to months of columns on whether he was the head of the world's first post-national country. In reality, Canadians have continued to try to forge some form of shared identity with varying levels of success.

Nearly twenty minutes into our conversation, we've now got poutines in front of us. Greenspot's poutine is very reliable, with dark gravy and chunky fries disappearing beneath large squeaky curds. We both give it a firm seal of approval. I mention some things I've learned over years of research, interviews and mulling the subject.

"Poutine is a different symbol from the others. It's clearly local, without clear cultural ties to France or other areas. It's also quintessentially modern, invented in the lifetimes of many people still alive today. Finally, it also reflects local customs," I tell him.

Cuthbertson interjects that just because he's rejected the appropriation label for a Wendy's poutine, or whatever else comes out of English-Canadian kitchens, that doesn't mean he thinks it should be Canadian.

"There's a reason why it can't be both. If it is Canadian, it can no longer serve as a marker of identity for Quebec. It can no longer be something that sets Quebec apart, something that makes it unique from the rest of Canada," he says.

"Are you guys full?" our waitress asks as she takes away two empty bowls that had contained poutine moments earlier. We both nod.

For the next several minutes, we talk about finding a balancing act that gives Quebec its due credit for poutine while allowing for something broader to happen going forward. "There will be some that will argue that it's appropriation," he says.

The problem with the idea of appropriation, which has become an increasingly loaded term in recent years, is that it requires something negative, a real harm or damage, according to Cuthbertson. "Hurt feelings that someone else is claiming your thing as their own doesn't cut it. That's why I don't know if I'd call what's happening with poutine 'appropriation,'" he adds.

"Is there real damage from English Canada claiming poutine as something greater than Quebec, as a Canadian dish?" I ask.

There's a long pause before Cuthbertson speaks again.

"You know, what sets poutine apart is that it's a uniquely modern symbol. We can talk about toques or ice hockey, but even if they were unique to Quebec, that was centuries ago. There was no wider Canada then because Quebec pretty much was Canada. But poutine is modern. It was invented and became popular with the upswell of Quebec nationalism and the Quiet Revolution. With the exception of the flag, what other modern symbol do we have as Quebecers? The Montreal Canadiens are too old, the flag isn't a symbol that can be claimed. Hydro-Quebec? How do you appropriate electricity? No. The one truly modern symbol is poutine. If others start claiming it as Canadian, there is some damage. It's lost."

After an hour, he's come fully around to the other side of the argument. "I hadn't thought of it that way before," he says. "It is appropriation."

One of the main criticisms of the concept of cultural appropriation is that it's often describing what some see as a positive exchange. The term is complex, confusing and often misapplied to activities as simple as just learning a different language or engaging with a different culture. There are examples of culture exchange that do seem positive. North American Chinese cuisine couldn't exist without a free flow of ideas between two cultures. However, in this case, the question isn't about the creation of something new from an exchange, but rather what label should be used to describe something created by one culture. Even anglophone Quebecers, like Cuthbertson, now seem to resist any greater Canadianization of poutine.

An example that's often brought up is pizza. As a dish, it's spread around the world and undergone an unfathomable amount of change. From the Chicago deep dish to a thin margarita pie, a pizza can be both recognizable and radically different. However, pizza remains Italian in origin.

Fabien-Ouellet's argument had been that calling a poutine "Canadian" would be like trying to recategorize a pizza as European. Sure, Italy is part of Europe, but it would do a deep disservice to the culture that created pizza—and likely leave patrons deeply confused—to open a shop selling "classic European pizza" or to mount a campaign to declare pizza as the official food of Europe. It also seems unlikely any food bureaucrats in Brussels would let that idea pass.

For those who might be dissatisfied with the conclusion from Fabien-Ouellet or Cuthbertson, I ask the latter if English Canada has a say going forward: "Noooo, they really don't. This isn't a discussion where they are invited."

As Cuthbertson leaves the Greenspot, I sit by the window staring at Montreal and think back to my earlier conversation with Fabien-Ouellet. In the half decade since he first wrote about the subject, he's concluded that the debate about poutine's national identity has been settled definitely in Quebec. "I think it's behind us. It's now well understood that poutine is Québécois and only Québécois," he told me. "We can now move forward in perfecting how we define Québécois and Canadian cuisine."

While the debate might be solved in Quebec, I asked him if any lasting cultural tension will be fed each time a foreign restaurateur puts a Canadian flag beside poutine on their menu. It's certainly not from malice. When she moved to Canada in her twenties, my German-born wife had no idea the country even had provinces—overseas chefs putting together a Canadian poutine would likely be in a similar position. It's something Fabien-Ouellet thinks about in his day job as a captain of Montreal's food scene.

"That would be a different dynamic. I was asked recently what we should do if someone promotes poutine in the United States with a Canadian flag. I concluded that we need to just explain that they made a choice to put a flag and they put the wrong flag. Why does it need a flag? Don't put any flag. Just serve poutine. But if you need a flag, put the correct one," he said.

I came away from my two conversations thinking that there's still quite a lot of work needed to get to the universal recognition that Quebecers aspire to see.

A few days after I spoke with Fabien-Ouellet, clue 96 for the *New York Times* Sunday crossword puzzle gave me a sense that things might be further along than I'd expected: "Québécois dish of french fries, cheese curds and gravy."

How poutine could take over the world

I PUT THE CAR IN PARK BECAUSE I CAN'T QUITE BELIEVE WHAT I'M seeing: "Poutine." It's there, in bright neon, advertised on the window of a burger restaurant near my house. There's even an illustration of a plate with fries, gravy and what looks like cheese curds—so I know this isn't some misunderstanding. The reason I'm surprised is that I'm nowhere near Canada. I'm on the outskirts of Wellington, New Zealand's capital city.

While living in Alberta, I met a New Zealander and got engaged, and she moved with me from my posting in Edmonton to one in Toronto, then back to Calgary. When she got offered a job in Wellington, it only seemed fair that I'd be the one who would follow her this time. We started building a new life a world away from poutine—and then one day a big neon sign loudly announced that there is no longer a world away from poutine.

I pull into the parking lot and walk into the BurgerFuel restaurant—it's one of New Zealand's largest fast-food chains—and I put in an order for poutine. Alongside the neon, I see that the menu promises a dish with "fries, hot gravy, fresh cheese curds, bacon and grated parmesan." The teenager behind the counter tells me the poutine comes back every year or so for a few months, but he doesn't know much beyond that. I'm unsure what to expect when he hands me a takeaway container that's warm to the touch. I head back to the car and open it up. It's unusual and looks nothing like a poutine you'd get at any restaurant in Quebec. It's messy beyond description. The curds are fully melted in little dairy puddles and speckled with bright bits of yellow parmesan. There's nothing in the cardboard box that a Canadian would recognize as a cheese curd. The bacon bits would be dry if they weren't also slowly sinking into the cheese like deck chairs from a doomed ocean liner. The pour of gravy is insufficiently generous, while the fries are somewhat overcooked and holding the entire thing together. It's a disaster area.

But then taste says a lot. Maybe it's the two years without a poutine talking, but I'm actually quite fond of it. It isn't trying to be a Quebec classic. It's thrown together to reflect local tastes. It's a Kiwi poutine and not promising to be anything else. For that, I give it a gold star for participation.

The most unfortunate thing about BurgerFuel's poutine, however—even worse than the cheese—is its name. The chain has decided to call its version of the dish a Vladimir Poutine. Frankly, the worst thing to happen to poutine in recent years is its unlikely association with Russian President Vladimir Putin. In French, the autocrat's family name is spelled *Poutine*. While that's ruined online search terms in French for the dish, there's worse. Soon after Russia's invasion of Ukraine in 2022, a poutine restaurant in Paris began receiving threatening phone calls. Some locals thought that La Maison de la Poutine, because of its name, was somehow glorifying Vladimir and the Russian state. The restaurant put out a very public and loud show of support for Ukraine—and engaged in a bit of poutine education.

While Quebec has a more understanding local population on the subject of poutine, and readily distinguishes between the two, the Roy Jucep also got caught up in the fervour following the invasion. It changed its online branding, removing all mention of poutine. It was now calling itself the inventor of "fries, cheese and gravy" to protest Russia's war. It was a more than symbolic change for the restaurant, given that its claim to fame, and the federal certificate on its wall, is specifically for its use of the word *poutine* to describe what it was serving. A year later, the Roy Jucep would revert to its "inventor of poutine" tagline without publicity.

Soon after Russian tanks began rumbling toward Kyiv, a Canadian doctor on Twitter launched an appeal for people around the world to get their Putin from their poutines straight: "One is a dangerous and unwholesome mix of greasy, lumpy and congealed ingredients. The other is a delicious food."

BurgerFuel isn't the only New Zealand restaurant to have added poutine to its menu in recent years. After hearing about more options out there, what else was I going to do while stuck on a small island country behind some of the world's strictest pandemic restrictions? Go for a drive. So I decide to go on another, much shorter quest to find a few of those poutines—but without my dad this time, who was over fourteen thousand kilometres and an unforgiving quarantine system away.

My first two attempts were duds, poutine at those restaurants being a seasonal dish, usually in the autumn. But then I stumbled into poutine while walking through the small city in central New Zealand where my wife's parents live. I happened on a poutine food truck in the parking lot of a local playground. Unfortunately, the Beaver and Bear was locked up for the day and I only had the menu to sustain me. The next time I visited the in-laws, the food truck was gone.

Undeterred, my final destination is the poutine that is most often described to me as New Zealand's best, and I'm guaranteed that it'll be there. It's at a restaurant called the Federal Delicatessen in downtown Auckland. Run by one of the country's most popular chefs, the Fed Deli has a "Montreal poutine" on its menu.

Stopping in with a friend, I found the Fed's fries wonderful, but its gravy was completely unsuitable for poutine and the cheese curds did not impress. I wrote a review of that Auckland poutine for my employer at the time, a local news website called *The Spinoff*. I described the deli's curds as mozzarella cut in cubes that slowly melted on the top. The morning after the story came out, I got a somewhat unhappy email from a senior member of the restaurant's staff who took issue with my description of the cheese. "Poutine is close to our hearts," he wrote, but they can't purchase Quebec-style cheese curds in New Zealand. While the country is absolutely awash in milk, with more cows than people, the appetite for eating fresh cheese just isn't there.

"Our cheese curds are made by a sheep farmer and cheesemaker named Miles. He makes them specifically for Federal Deli. So they are a cheese curd, not mozzarella. They are as authentic and as close to the Canadian experience as we can create in li'l old NZ," I was told by email.

I called Miles on his farm, listed in the phone book, and waited as I heard him being called in from the fields for a chat. As he explained it, he'd promised he could "throw together cheese curds with a good melting and stringy texture." There was a process of trial and error to get "a good bit of squeak" out of the cheese. I was left impressed by the amount of effort that had gone into creating cheese curds for a single restaurant.

New Zealanders I spoke with described poutine as something quintessentially Canadian and wonderful. The Auckland deli's use of Montreal to describe poutine, while incorrect, seemed an honest attempt to link the dish to the only city in Quebec most of them had ever heard of. I got to thinking about the debate back home on how poutine should be presented to the world. The words of Annie Barsalou at La Banquise kept coming back to me, with her attempt to navigate Canada's founding nations and her exasperation at any strife over identity. Poutine is now the closest thing Canada has to a national dish, and that includes the offerings from all provinces and territories. Quebecers will always know that they invented poutine, and the people of Drummondville will always know, deep down in that incredible well of civic pride, that they have some of the best in the world. But sitting in Auckland, that seemed very far away.

The feeling wasn't going to last long.

A decade after I left Quebec for English Canada and then New Zealand, I came back permanently. My wife and I had decided we wanted to make Quebec our home. When I told my dad on the phone, he was overjoyed. I came back to a Quebec that seemed more French, more successful and even more proud of its culture than the one I'd left years earlier. It took months to wipe the smile off my face from the small daily joys that came from living in Montreal again after so many years away. My wife threw herself into French classes, and while our golden retriever still hasn't mastered French commands, he doesn't really get English ones that aren't spoken in a thick New Zealand accent.

Having not seen my father in several years, except for the odd video call where we'd kept up a pretty solid banter on the Montreal Canadiens and poutine, it was time for a visit. Soon after we got settled, I headed back to Trois-Rivières. What better way to get back into the groove of things than to go for one more drive down the poutine highway, I thought.

I walk through the unlocked front door of my childhood home and find my dad where he'd so often been, sitting at the kitchen counter with a newspaper and the TV on in the background. He is a little older, greyer and slower as he walks over, nearly in his eighties at this point. "*La grosse visite*," he says excitedly, getting up from his chair.

After a bit of chitchat, we head out to his car and drive back over the Laviolette Bridge away from Trois-Rivières, the giant span's green paint peeling in different places than it had been years earlier, but peeling all the same. Some of the same stories come out as we drive, but I hear new ones about his youth too. "Everything has changed so much," he tells me, pointing to new businesses. "But we still have poutine."

In his old town, he blows through a stop sign, deep in reflection. Minutes later we're rolling at walking speed down a rural highway, the words just spilling out of him.

"I'm getting a little tired. Do you mind if we head back to my place?" he asks.

"Of course not." I offer to drive but he waves the words away after he turns around. It's a quick drive back, and a few blocks before his house he asks if I'm hungry.

"Absolutely. What do you have in mind?" I ask. He says nothing.

We pull up at a Fromagerie Victoria not far from where he lives. My dad comes here most days of the week, to sit with a group of friends, drink bottomless cups of drip coffee and chat. He wants to talk about that day when we visited the *fromagerie* where he worked so many years ago. "Before that visit, I hadn't thought about those guys in decades. I was just a kid then, eighteen. Nearly that entire gang is dead now. Boudreau, Gaudette, Savard. All dead. All the guys who made the cheese with me. A lot of those guys drank—a lot. They didn't give themselves much of a chance. Had I kept going the way I was, I'd probably be in the same place as them." He stares out in the distance. "I drank from the age of seventeen until I was about fifty-five. I stopped in January 1999. I'd spent enough time doing that, doing enough foolish things."

"A classic poutine for Laurent," a voice says over a loudspeaker. There had been no debate, almost no real discussion, about what we'd eat when we came in.

"I'll get that," I tell him. Walking over to the counter, I'm thinking of what to say next. I hadn't meant for our poutine conversations to turn into big talks, but they have. I've never asked my dad about his drinking. It wasn't so much taboo as we didn't talk about it. How do you ask? What do you ask? But he'd been sober for two decades, so this might be as good a time as any.

I take a deep breath, put the poutine down on the table and look at him. "Why did you drink?" I ask.

There's a long delay and a shrug. "I was stuck inside myself and had trouble expressing myself. When I drank a beer, I woke up a bit. I wasn't able to speak to a girl, but with a beer I could. I couldn't ask a girl to dance with me, but with a beer I could. So you end up going to the bar every night and drinking every night. You end up... addicted to it," he says, looking lost in thought. "That's the problem of most alcoholics. Many have had trauma as children. They're stuck and start drinking to help express themselves better."

"Okay, but you never had a trauma," I say. The silence lingers.

"Well, when I was two, I was in a coma for two days." He stops and looks at me. "I'd taken a bottle of pills from my mother. No one knows that. Your mother doesn't even know that. My mother was pregnant with my sister and she was really sick, so the doctor had given her some pills. She'd gone to see a cousin who was a priest in Montreal, so we had a babysitter who came to help. My little brother was only eleven months old. At a certain point, my father needed some help in the barn. One of our cows was giving birth and he needed an extra hand. She told him, 'If I come and help, I'll be leaving the kids alone in the house.' He told her not to worry, it would only take fifteen minutes.

"There was one rule at our house at the time: we couldn't go into our parents' room. It was completely forbidden. So what did I do the moment she left? I went right into my parents' room. There was a little box of pills on a side table. Back in those days, you got pills in a small brown cardboard box, like candies. When I opened the box, the pills looked like Smarties. They were bitter, so the doctor had wrapped the pills in chocolate. I sat there and started sucking off the chocolate, and when it got too bitter, I swallowed the pill. I probably swallowed about a dozen, and the pills took effect. I was two years old. Boom, I fell unconscious. They found the pillbox on the floor, with pills everywhere and a dozen missing.

"When the babysitter came back to the house to see what was going on, she saw that the door was slightly open to my parents' room. She pushed on the door but it wouldn't move. I'd fallen behind it and my body was blocking it. I only weighed about twenty pounds, so she pushed me out of the way and found me unconscious. I was breathing, but my eyes were rolled all the way back. She ran to the barn and told my father that I was on the floor and wasn't moving. He ran in, saw me and called the doctor. It was mid-January and a big snowstorm had just shut down all the local roads. The doctor told my father he would go look for one of the two snowmobiles in the village. He eventually found one and arrived three hours later. When my father had first called, he'd said to put me in a big metal wash bin and fill it with snow, and the two of them were rubbing me with snow. My temperature was through the roof. I'd started to stabilize when the doctor arrived, and he told my dad, 'If he lives through the night, he'll be fine. But how he'll be up in his head, mentally, I don't know.'"

He looks at my poutine. "You should eat before it's cold," he says.

I shake my head. "You've always known that happened?" I ask him.

"No, I haven't known this story for very long. I ran into the baby-sitter a few years ago at a funeral. My father had never told me a word about any of this. No one told me. I grew up, I got married and no one said anything. I was at the funeral home, talking with a cousin when the babysitter came up to me. 'You're Charles's boy?' she asked. I look a lot like my dad. I nodded. 'You're Laurent, the oldest one? You gave me quite a fright when you were a child.' She then told me the entire story, right there in the middle of the funeral home."

He takes a deep breath and spears a cheese curd with his fork. He slowly chews it, and his eyes are red when he looks up at me again.

"After two days, I opened my eyes. I couldn't see, I couldn't hear, I couldn't talk and I couldn't walk. It all slowly came back, but it took four months for me to relearn how to walk. And after that, I was afraid of everything. My room was on the second floor. I had been able to go up the stairs before, but now my dad had to pick me up and bring me upstairs. When the neighbours came over to visit, I'd hide in the bathroom. And this I do remember—when my uncle used to visit, he'd say, 'I think one of them is missing.' He knew the situation, and I'd be hiding in the bathroom or behind the stove. That was two years later. I remember doing that and my uncle saying that. I also remember being afraid of the stairs, but I didn't remember why. Now I know. That fear always stayed with me. It was hard for me to communicate with strangers. I think that's why I would drink. It was a magic remedy."

There are tears streaming down my face. I remember that I'd asked him to speak at my wedding, but he'd very politely and firmly said no. He didn't want to. I'd never understood why. Now, I did.

"Then my mother died during those years when I was a child. She had two children in a row who each died a month after coming home. I was sensitive to that. All the bad stuff in the world just stuck to me. That was a rough bit." He looks off in the distance. "I never told anyone."

A family with boisterous children takes a seat at a nearby table. We both enjoy a momentary interruption as the kids announce how happy they are that poutine is on the way.

"It's funny that my dad never told me about this. He must have felt guilty. If he hadn't asked the babysitter to come to the barn, it wouldn't have happened. The babysitter told me I was quite a handful before that day. I used to run and scream and smile, like a normal kid. After that, there was none of that. I stopped speaking for a long time. I never ran, screamed or smiled much as a kid after that."

Had I not asked about his drinking, I would have never learned that he's been quietly piecing together his own childhood over the past few years.

"That's my story, I guess." He wipes away some tears. I don't know what to do. I hold his hand and then we get up and I give him a hug. We pack up what's left of the poutine.

"You started a family and raised two kids. There's a lot more to your story," I say to him. "But knowing what happened to you, and about your drinking, helps me understand a lot about my childhood. It wasn't always easy... This really helps me understand."

We get into his car and he starts driving home. "Yes, and I didn't have an easy childhood either. A few months after my mother died, my father had a bad car accident. He was drunk one night, and he fell asleep and drove into the front of another car. He had to go to the hospital in Montreal for months because his left arm was ripped off. I was eight years old and alone at the farm with my two younger brothers and my sister. I was expected to take over the farm. We had over twenty cows, we had pigs, we had a chicken coop."

There's a long moment of silence. The emotions are bubbling below the surface. I'm trying to hold it together. We're both looking forward out the car window. He's an eight-year-old, he's still afraid of strangers and his life has been surrounded by death. The stretch of road where he's telling me this story is now burned into my memory. I knew his childhood was tough. This is something else.

"What do you mean?" That's all I can manage to say.

"Well, I had to take over the farm and I couldn't do it. I was just eight. I tried. It was hard work with all the animals and also looking after my brothers and sister. The family had to shut down the farm until my dad could come back." His voice is absolutely breaking, not with self-pity or sadness at what he was expected to do, but with regret. The sting of failure. Over seven decades later, he still has that little boy inside of him who was asked to do the impossible and couldn't. "I tried but I failed. It was just too much work for me."

He and his brothers and sister spent the next year being shuffled between family members who could look after them. They went to three different schoolhouses in one year. Occasionally, they'd go past the old family farm, the lights off and weeds growing in the fields. They were, in effect, orphans for a year after suddenly losing their mother and then their father to a long recovery. My granddad, who died just before I was born, eventually was cleared medically to go home and look after his children and care for the farm again, but my dad wasn't the same. He was still recovering from his earlier incident, with trauma that meant he still felt the urge to run behind the stove and hide when a stranger came to the door. He's never shared any of this before.

I repeat to him how it wasn't his fault, he'd been given an impossible task, but he just looks at me. He's still grappling with it all himself. I spend the rest of our drive quietly going through the tape of my own childhood with him, revisiting old conclusions about why things had happened the way they had. I now see quite differently his trouble connecting with me and the difficulty he had seeing his own son going away all those years before. It feels like quicksand has opened beneath years of memories.

We get out of the car at his place and I give him another hug. We're both exhausted. "I'll see you tomorrow," he tells me and goes inside.

I drive over to his house the next morning and find him in a good mood. "It was good to talk about that," he tells me. "Oh, and I forgot to tell you, I got an offer on the house. Some Moroccan family is going to buy it. I accepted."

"Congratulations. When are you going to sell? What's the plan?"

"I'm going to move out of here on July 1. My friend has a place for me in an apartment building where he lives. *Un cinq-et-demi,*" he tells me. That makes sense: July 1 is Quebec's moving day and a three-bedroom apartment, a five-and-a-half in the local lingo, is a nice entry into the rental world for someone who has had a large bungalow to himself for over a decade.

"But we need to finish the poutine story," he tells me. He's happy. My emotions are all over the place. My childhood home is being sold. It's been a taxing few days. There's also the emotional upheaval of learning that your dad isn't quite who you thought he was—he's far more complex and surprisingly happy and well-rounded considering what he's overcome. He's also dealing with unburdening himself for the first time in decades, of both the troubles on his mind and his longtime home.

"Wait. You sold the house?" I ask, my mind only now catching up with everything he just told me.

"Yes. But not today. Tell me the story," he says.

I take the hint. In recent months, I'd been doing research and interviewing people to stitch together the last parts of the poutine narrative.

"Okay, let me tell you what I learned about how poutine got from Quebec to the rest of Canada, and then around the world," I tell him.

"That sounds perfect," he answers. We both want the warm comfort of poutine.

Around the time I was born in the 1980s, poutine jumped across the Ottawa River into Ontario. The *New York Times,* of all places, had a story in 1988 about a new dish that was gaining popularity in the logging town of Pembroke, north of Ottawa. Chip trucks were all the rage in the Ottawa Valley and, as the newspaper reported, "crisp double-cooked chips, or french fries, sprinkled with salt and doused with white vinegar, are the trucks' mainstays, but chips with gravy and chips with cheese and gravy are gaining in popularity. Here, any occasion is an excuse for buying chips, whether as a snack after a hockey game or before lunch." A year later, the newspaper mentioned poutine in a travel piece for northern Vermont, describing poutine by name for the first time as something to get right across the border, a "peculiarly Quebec snack of french fries mixed with pale curds of cheddar."

Poutine's first foothold outside of Quebec is with little doubt the Ottawa Valley. Even before Annie Barsalou took over La Banquise, poutine had followed the tendril of highways near what's known in Quebec as the Rivière des Outaouais into the string of rural communities between Montreal and Ottawa. Through chip wagons and hockey games, poutine travelled between the English and French towns on either side of the river.

Poutine didn't stay at just the roadside joints for long. A company that was only a few years old decided to get in on the action. New York Fries started opening restaurants in the Ottawa area, and poutine was added to the menu locally for the first time in 1990.

"When you opened up a store in Ottawa then, you just had to have poutine on the menu," Craig Burt tells me. He's now the head of New York Fries, but he'd only joined the chain the year before, in 1989. He remembers those first days well. "We started selling it and it went like gangbusters."

Poutine's first lasting home beyond the Quebec border and its French-speaking periphery, as far as I can tell, is not where you'd expect. "It was Newmarket, Ontario," Burt tells me. "Which is probably the strangest place on the planet to start introducing poutine." A New York Fries franchisee in the suburb north of Toronto had seen poutine gaining traction during a visit to eastern Ontario and wanted to give it a go. Only a few months after the Ottawa-area stores added poutine to their rotation, he volunteered to bring poutine closer to English Canada's largest market. It was still 1990.

There would be no need to repeat the same trials faced by Ashton Leblond and his Chez Ashton restaurant two decades earlier. Newmarket didn't need to be convinced that the Quebec dish with the odd name was worth trying—the restaurant quickly sold out. Other New York Fries operators wanted in, and the rollout was spectacularly fast from there. Within a year, poutine was on the chain's menu across Canada. Poutine may have experienced a rough ride in the English-Canadian press and among its tastemakers, but the stomachs of Canadians needed no coaxing.

"I've never eaten at New York Fries," my dad tells me, as I'm walking him through the story.

"I think I had it in Calgary once," I tell him.

While English Canada loved poutine, something different in anglophone taste quickly became apparent. "I remember this distinctly: they wanted the cheese curd melted," says Burt. There's a long pause in our conversation. I'm flabbergasted—this is like admitting you prefer your beer warm. "The consumers didn't like the squeaky cheese. They didn't understand it. They wanted their curd melted, so we had to do it for them."

He partly explains the two solitudes of squeak by describing a greater and distinctly American influence over English Canada's food. With more culinary experience with mozzarella cheese melted over fries and sandwiches, English Canadians were more comfortable with melted cheese. "I tried to explain it to customers. I would tell them, 'You know, they're not supposed to be melted.' 'No, no, I want them melted' was always the reply. Next thing you know, we're melting them," Burt says, giving off the sense that he'd had to accept what seemed like blasphemy even to himself.

New York Fries was getting big, chunky, moist curds, which are absolutely perfect for a poutine in Quebec. But to please tastes in Ontario, restaurant staff spent hours working slicers, cutting curds into small bits that were then frozen to remove the moisture. The resulting curd would melt under hot gravy. To this exact moment in my conversation with Burt, I'd thought that English Canada's usually less-than-spectacular poutine was a consequence of complicated logistics and the difficulty of sourcing local curd. While that's still true in some locations, English-Canadian consumers have made it easy on many poutine restaurants by preferring a dry husk of curd. Over three decades later, tastes haven't changed.

Quebec's curds aren't exactly a monolith either. Over the lifetime since poutine hit the menu at the Roy Jucep, some loose regional distinctions have emerged. Diners in Quebec City still prefer a big, moist curd. Plates at Chez Ashton are still topped by chunks of cheesy moisture, glistening in the restaurant's neon lights. The chain's workers, wearing their tall fabric wedge hats, wouldn't dream of chopping up a cheese curd. Farther south, there's no such thing as a Montreal style of poutine, and that city's restaurants are increasingly inconsistent when it comes to their curds. Admittedly, some are also just not that good.

While La Banquise continues to lean heavily on moist curds that pop, other institutions have edged toward the English taste. It's not clear if that's just because it's easier to skimp on curds or due to customer demand. Chez Claudette, a colourful greasy spoon near the city's trendy Mile End neighbourhood, often appears on lists of where to go when La Banquise's lines have grown too long—it's hard to overstate how long the lines can become. With far less polish and more grit, Chez Claudette does have that authentic feel. However, its curds were cold and dry when I visited, melting on my poutine. Burt, who has eaten as much poutine as any other expert, tells me that Montreal is different when it comes to curds. The willingness to put up with a melted mess falling off your fork is likely a reflection of the city's English heritage.

Burt found himself in the right place at the right time to guide poutine's Canadian growth. While he doesn't speak French, he was born in Sherbrooke, Quebec, and grew up in Drummondville. His family on both sides goes back generations in the Eastern Townships, not far from Ashton Leblond's hometown. His family left Quebec for Ontario right before poutine became a firmly installed comfort food, but cheese curds left an indelible mark on his childhood. "Right by our chalet was a dairy farm, and the guy produced his own cheese curds. On the weekends, we'd go up and grab a fresh bowl that would absolutely blow your mind," he reminisces.

Despite its American name, New York Fries is a fully Canadian operation. As poutine grew in importance for the chain, Burt headed back to his roots to find a way of anchoring the restaurant's star dish closer to its cultural heritage. A year after poutine spread across all its Canadian stores, the brand began purchasing its cheese curds from Quebec. Fromagerie La Chaudière in the small town of Lac-Mégantic supplies them. It makes smaller curds for the English restaurants, which melt quickly in the gravy that is kept at a higher temperature for the purpose.

The brand has spread around the world in recent years. You can buy a poutine from New York Fries in Dubai, Panama and a number of other countries. The next big step is expansion to the US. "Poutine will be front and centre as we launch there. It's not so big in the US. Poutine is kind of a niche thing—you only find it in some mid- or high-end restaurants. It's few and far between. So hey, maybe we can start something," he says.

To supply all those stores, Burt needs a lot of potatoes. Who better to explain the making of a humble fry than the guy who runs New York Fries? Most of the potatoes for the chain's Canadian restaurants are from

New Brunswick. A mix of farming know-how and technology is required to ensure restaurants get the right potatoes. For you tuber enthusiasts out there, the right potato most of the year is a Russet Burbank. It's the expected choice, the standard potato. Picture a brown potato in your head and you're likely thinking of a Russet Burbank. It's literally the emoji potato. It's also the most popular potato in North America, with a nutty, sort of earthy flavour that helps create a light-tasting fry.

Staff at the restaurants start most days cutting potatoes into fries. They're washed, cut and put in water. It is the start of a surprisingly long process for what most people think of as food-court fare. The freshly cut fries are then racked and dried. In total, they'll be cooked three times. It takes about a half-hour to cook each batch, with drying and racking between each cooking period. The idea is to cook them on the inside before the outside. The final trip to the cooking oil, which lasts just under a minute, gets the fresh fries hot for a waiting customer.

There is a bit of a problem with the company's choice of potato. One part of the country doesn't really like the Russet Burbank as a french fry—and of course, it's Quebec. Instead of light, crispy fries, the province prefers something that's thicker, heavier and far more salted. The resulting fries are often thick-cut, droopy and brown, more soft than snappy. Many of the province's *casse-croûtes* try to recreate the taste from decades ago, when fries were submerged in beef tallow and bacon fat.

Faced with a need for different curds and fries, English Canada's poutine brands struggle in Quebec. The province's food economy is also more local and operates half a step outside the Canadian mainstream. When it comes to poutine, taste profiles have diverged between Quebec and the rest of the country. There are no melted curds here— restaurants need fresh, local cheese. English Canada's beefy-tasting gravy is replaced by Quebec's preference for barbecue chicken flavour. And the fries need to fit local tastes.

Despite poutine's central place on the New York Fries menu across the country and its quick adoption by many diners, it took nearly two decades for it to really become a national dish. There were a number of points along the way when English Canada wasn't quite sure what to do with poutine. With the dish now deracinated, should it still adhere to that classic Quebec recipe? Should it be loaded up with chili and other toppings? Things stayed fairly stagnant and sales plateaued outside Quebec. Then, all of a sudden, everything changed.

Seen in retrospect, 2010 was the watershed year for poutine. It's the year when poutine became Canada's dish for millions of people. English Canadians also came around to what people in Drummondville had long known: you can't beat a classic poutine. What happened? The Vancouver Olympics.

"It was a real shift in the poutine business. It just went boom, because everybody was talking about it," Burt tells me. "Canada was on the international stage and we just rode this wave of interest in poutine. There was all of this hype about poutine. This 'new Canadian dish' was on all the American news shows. It went crazy. Anything with cheese curd on it sold. People were just grasping for it all of a sudden."

Ryan Smolkin didn't know it at the time, but he was part of the national poutine wave building around the 2010 Winter Olympics. Fourteen months before Wayne Gretzky carried a torch through downtown Vancouver to light the Olympic cauldron, Smolkin opened the first restaurant in a chain he was launching. Smoke's Poutinerie opened its doors on Adelaide Street West in downtown Toronto. A short walk from the city's theatre district and Roy Thomson Hall, Smoke's would bring Quebec-style poutine to Canada's largest city.

It's hard to miss Smoke's when you see it now. The chain's locations across Canada are decked out in bright red plaid, and its mascot, known simply as Smoke, is plastered everywhere, rendered in black and white, with big nerdy glasses, a messy mop of hair and a constant grin. Think Bob Ross in computer-programmer chic. There's no mistaking the brand as very Canadian and for Canadians.

Ryan Smolkin died in October 2023 from complications following surgery. He was fifty. He was described by friends as sometimes quiet and reserved, except for when he was the focus of attention. Smolkin turned his persona to maximum when we spoke. I'm grateful for it.

It's December 2022 and I've reached Smolkin on Zoom while he's at the company's headquarters in the Toronto suburb of Ajax. He's as much of a character as Smoke the mascot. He's loud, colourful and swears constantly during our hour-long conversation.

To set the scene, he's dressed in the company's trademark red plaid, in a room decked out in red plaid, surrounded by red plaid swag. "It's just a little bit of plaid. The global headquarters! Just a little plaidified," he says with a chuckle. "We even plaidified our storage crates and shit… We've got to fire it up, baby!" He's approached this chat with the energy of a wrestling promoter, and he rarely falters.

There are certainly larger restaurant chains than Smoke's that sell poutine— McDonald's serves the dish across Canada now—but I'm talking to Smolkin because of his dedication to poutine and all the different ways it can be made. "I created a poutinerie. Nothing but poutine. Just poutine. Just loaded poutine. Just piled high. That's. All. I. Fucking. Serve," he tells me.

Send the kids to bed. Welcome to the world of Smoke's.

The idea to start a dedicated poutinerie first came to Smolkin in the early 2000s. His background is in advertising, and he tells me that he knew from the start the only way a poutine chain could work is through strong branding. At the centre of it would be an invented mascot: Smoke. "I put the brand around him and the famous face. Smoke himself, the legend. It's about more than the poutine and it's more than Quebec and it's more than Canada. Even though we've conquered

Canada and we've got a shitload of locations. What about the other seven or eight billion people on the planet?"

For those overseas who haven't got much of a clue what poutine is, Smolkin pitches it as a form of messy loaded fries. Everyone understands messy fries, he tells me. "In our case, it's got that base of fries, curds and gravy. Then load just anything else you want on top of it. Around the world, everywhere you go, it's loaded fries. Number one food in the fucking world, I'd say."

As part of his pre-opening travels, he went on a research trip to Quebec to figure out what kind of poutine joint he should create. He had a long list of restaurants to visit, including one in Montreal that has stuck with him. "It was an awesome summer, just unbelievable. You know La Banquise? I saved that one until the end. That one I remember well. I went on a Wednesday night. It's, like, three in the morning, it's pouring rain and I lined up at the doors with the masses. I was like, 'Holy fuck, this is damn good. I'm onto something huge. This is going to be unbelievable.' I already was building in downtown TO, but when I saw that, I knew. You go in there and the full menu is poutine and people are just ordering poutine at that time of night. So I remember thinking, 'This is it, baby. Global domination!' I'm a businessperson, not a restaurateur. I was seeing a business opportunity. But I love my poutine and this is for life."

Smolkin unlocked the doors on the first Smoke's location at 11:30 a.m. He relocked them about two hours later. The restaurant had run out of nearly everything. He'd spent the previous months spreading Smoke's face through Toronto. Armed with a minuscule advertising budget—he says about $20, and it's not clear if he's serious about the amount—he'd printed hundreds of small stickers of Smoke and plastered the city with them. Torontonians spent months surrounded by all the black-and-white stickers of the mascot as a rock star, ballerina, lover, fighter and more. It became close to impossible to travel the city without seeing Smoke's grin. I was in university in Montreal at the time and can still clearly remember those stickers appearing nearly everywhere. There was also a lot of confusion and interest in whatever it was.

"Everybody knew the face. Then they put two and two together. When we opened up, it was lined up a mile long around the block," he says with a laugh. "There was more excitement and opportunity than I thought there'd be. It's also been more work than I thought it would be. I've built companies over the years, but it was pretty insane how crazy it got."

On that first day, the only thing they didn't run out of were potatoes. Workers got down to peeling in a back room, but you can't run a fast-food restaurant with just potatoes. Smolkin flipped the sign over to "closed" and headed to the grocery store. "I went down to the Loblaws and cleared out the whole bacon section. Like, $450 worth of bacon that I had in the cart. I threw that on the belt to put it through and all these people are looking at me like, 'Who's this fucking idiot?' Then we were blanching fries back at the office, we got the gravy ready and we opened again at five o'clock. It was pretty intense."

His plan that first day was to stay open late like La Banquise and make poutine until dawn. He now admits that was a tad cocky. By 9 p.m., they'd run out of supplies again and closed for the night. The second day, he only managed to keep the restaurant open for four hours. The learning curve was steep, and it would take months to figure out how to run the place like he wanted.

"Nights were always going to be my core business. We were insane during the days. We opened up the first late night and it's dead," he admits, the Don Cherry-esque fight draining from his voice. "At ten o'clock, it's dead. Midnight, it's dead. And then 1:30 a.m. comes in. Boom! There it is, baby! That 1:30 a.m. to 3:30 a.m. window. The masses lined up at the door, down the stairs, around the block."

After that first Smoke's Poutinerie hit its stride, Smolkin added more locations quickly. There was a poutine gold rush on across Canada, as restaurants and chains embraced the dish and added it to menus following the Vancouver Olympics in 2010. The chain kept growing over the following decade and, by the end of 2019, Smoke's had opened 150 locations around the world. Most of those were in Canada and there was a location in nearly every province. Quebec was an exception—franchisees had tried and failed a few times to make it in the province of poutine's birth.

With restaurants under construction across Europe and the Middle East, alongside plans being hatched for massive expansion in Asia with new franchisees, it looked like 2020 was going to be poutine's breakthrough international year. Then COVID-19 hit. The restaurant chains retreated to Canada as the world went into lockdown and supply chains snarled, expansion plans froze up and locations closed. But poutine will still have its day around the world, Smolkin assures me.

One thing sets Smoke's apart from other chains selling poutine, and it's something noteworthy. It's the cheese curds. He's faced complaints about the squeak and lack of melting in the past, but Smolkin is unwilling to compromise. He's passionate, deeply passionate, about his cheese curds. "Oh my God, I slap people around. It's got to squeak! You get these people who complain that it's not melting. They think there's something wrong with it. It's not melting because it's *fresh, real cheese curd from Quebec*, you fucking idiots!" His voice is nearly trembling by the end of that sentence, which could be punctuated with more exclamation marks for how often the audio needle of our conversation is shooting into the red.

He's cagey about how he's seemingly broken the challenge of distributing fresh cheese curds across Canada. All the chain's curds come from Maison Riviera, a *fromagerie* about forty-five minutes east of Montreal. He says the two have a deep partnership that includes a number of "processes invented to help with longevity." A cursory examination of Riviera's curds, available at grocery stores in Quebec, shows that they are slightly lower in fat and have considerably more moisture than average. Though that doesn't really explain how he can get curds to British Columbia that are still moist and squeaky. Smolkin then adds that the Quebec curds are sent to all the chain's restaurants. Does he freeze and then warm them again? He won't explain. "I can't reveal my secrets and that's one of my key secrets," he says, quite seriously for the first time. I write in my notepad: *What is it about these poutine businessmen and their secrets?*

Canada doesn't have much of a culinary identity abroad, when it does at all, beyond maple syrup. To push poutine toward a more global future, Smolkin wants to more closely link it to its Canadian identity. But not exactly the Canada that's quiet, polite and into peacekeeping. Instead, he says we should use the opportunity to "change the perception of Canada. Bigger, bolder, louder." Move it toward Smoke's, in other words.

One thing that might stand in the way of a maple leaf–clad poutine is Quebecers who view the dish as a lasting and indivisible symbol of that province's heritage. For the thinkers like Nicolas Fabien-Ouellet who have questioned whether anyone is still trying to claim a Canadian identity for poutine, Ryan Smolkin is their foil. But he just waves aside the question. He says he has no time for the Quebec versus Canada debate.

"While they're fighting over who invented it and what to do with it, I'm going to take the Canadian classic, load everything I can think of on top of it and take it to the rest of the world. They can argue, that doesn't bother me. But it's not about where you're buying it, it's about who's making it best. Just because I don't live in Quebec, that doesn't mean I don't make a really good poutine."

As the dish spreads, could there come a point in the future where the world's best poutine isn't in Quebec and isn't in Canada?

"Yeah, maybe," Smolkin responds with a shrug. There's a very long pause. "Ha! No. Never."

The perfect food

THE FIRST QUESTION I GOT ASKED BY NEARLY EVERYONE WHILE I was researching this book was the same: "Where's the best poutine?" The second was invariably about where poutine is from, a question that's been thoroughly explored at this point. So where should you go for a good dish?

Despite eating a lot of poutine in my lifetime, answering that first question remains difficult. So much of any answer is wrapped up in personal preference and nostalgia. I will nearly always order a classic poutine, and I'm looking for the freshest cheese. The fries and gravy are the arenas where a chef can surprise and delight.

The most honest answer is that my favourite poutine is the one I often had with my friends when I was a teenager in Trois-Rivières. The restaurant we'd order from is still around, and I head back every few years to recapture that taste. It's the one poutine I compare every other poutine to. It's my standard measure. And admittedly, each time I go back to it and dig into the mess in that deep bowl, it's never as good as I remember—as you'd expect of anything you are revisiting from the prime of your teenage years. It fails to meet its own test. The cheese doesn't squeak as loudly, the fries are too soft, the gravy too plain.

If you didn't grow up in Quebec and don't have a mythical poutine of your youth that you can remember fondly, all is not lost. There's a lot of bad poutine in this world—here's how I try to steer clear of it. Montreal has some great poutine, but the odds of finding mind-blowing poutine in the city are not in your favour. Leave Montreal, explore the Québécois culture that created poutine and look for a roadside restaurant or *casse-croûte* with a busy parking lot. You'll find one reliably enough with just a little bit of driving beyond the metropolis. Six decades after poutine emerged from fry shack culture, that's still where you'll find the exemplars of poutine done right. At a time when poutine has become big business with fortunes attached to it, these small shops are still where poutine makes hearts beat hardest. Roll up your sleeves and enjoy.

I have stopped, spontaneously, at a number of unassuming *casse-croûtes* on rural roads that have absolutely shaken me with fantastic poutine. I've also gone to highly recommended poutine joints in Quebec's bigger cities that aren't worth mentioning.

If you're sure you've found a great poutine, the best poutine, that's wonderful. Enjoy that feeling, and dig into it. Now, prepare to debate the people around you. Arguing about poutine is a full-contact verbal sport in Quebec in which no one gets hurt. To be sure, there are wrong answers to the question of where to find the best poutine, but there really aren't any collective right ones. The best poutine can be yours alone.

While I've come to some firm conclusions on poutine's history, it's certainly possible pieces of evidence have eluded me. The discussion over who came first likely won't end anytime soon, if only because it's so enjoyable to so many people. I recently mentioned poutine while sitting in the chair at my barbershop in the Hochelaga-Maisonneuve neighbourhood of Montreal. An absolutely ferocious debate erupted over where the first poutine came from. Everyone in the room got involved. One man argued it was Victoriaville, another said it was somewhere near Sherbrooke. I mentioned Drummondville and a young barber threateningly—jokingly—held up his scissors and declared my ideas suspect. "This is what happens when someone mentions poutine," my barber Adam told me as he got back to cutting, the maelstrom carrying on around us. "Look what you've done." There was as much argument filling the shop as there was chopped hair on the floor.

Two decades into the twenty-first century, poutine has begun to develop a truly global reach as a Canadian delicacy. There have even been poutine classes held in Pyongyang, the capital of North Korea. Poutine opens doors. Where it was once seen as synonymous with backwardness and rural Quebec, poutine as a name and plate is now recognizable around the world as a symbol for Canada—and Quebec for those who are in the know. That's no small feat for something so simple.

Roy Oh called it the "perfect dish." Many will scoff at that characterization. Even I laughed when I heard him say it. Reflecting more on it, I realized there is something to poutine that is extraordinary. Perhaps it's the ease with which you can share it. You can easily split a poutine with family, old friends and new acquaintances. It's a savoury and satisfying icebreaker, a cure for division when people are pulling apart. Quebec and Canada have an amazing dish, and the world wants more poutine.

When I first set out to discover poutine with my father, I thought we'd learn about cheese curds and potatoes. I thought there might be a story there, but mostly, I expected we'd eat a lot of poutine. That came quickly and enjoyably enough. We met an unforgettable cast of characters and drove to parts of Quebec I hadn't visited yet. I began to appreciate Quebec and its culture in ways I hadn't known I was missing previously. The pieces were all there from my childhood, and they suddenly came together in new ways.

What I hadn't expected was what would happen between each serving of poutine. I began enjoying my time with my father—not for the food but for what I was learning about him. I thought I'd known him before we set out on the poutine highway—I did not. I don't know how else I would have come to know the man he is and the challenges he's faced without that shared poutine in front of us, as we pushed aside our timidity with each bite.

Acknowledgements

THIS BOOK WOULD NOT HAVE BEEN POSSIBLE WITHOUT THE HELP of the many people within its pages who gave their time generously to answer my many questions on curds and life in Quebec. That includes my dad, Laurent Lamothe, who set off on a drive to find a poutine or two and ended up sharing his story. Thanks, Dad.

I would not have been able to write about poutine without the early support of *The Globe and Mail*. The idea for the original article, "Poutine on the side," which would eventually become this book, was hatched at a table in the back of a Toronto bar with Dennis Choquette, Gabe Gonda and Sinclair Stewart. Literary agents John Pearce and Chris Casuccio at Westwood Creative Artists helped refine that idea into what you're reading today. Finally, the team at Douglas and McIntyre—Anna Comfort O'Keeffe, Caroline Skelton, Pam Robertson, Jen Lauriault and Ariel Brewster—provided support, invaluable edits and the occasional nudge.

I was travelling through Quebec conducting research—eating poutine—for this book when the Covid pandemic struck. I'd like to thank Giuseppe Valiante for letting me work from his kitchen table, and share his Scotch, when the world locked down and I was stranded.

Finally, none of this would have been possible without the incredible support of my wife, Mirjam, who didn't blink when we uprooted our lives four times for continental moves, raised a dog and gave birth to our son, Elio, in less time than it took me to write this.

About the author

BORN IN THE HEART OF RURAL QUEBEC, JUSTIN GIOVANNETTI Lamothe has worked as a journalist in Ontario, Alberta and British Columbia. His reporting has focused on the human drama at the centre of such major events as the rail disaster in Lac-Mégantic and the wildfires in Fort McMurray, and has earned him an investigative award from the Canadian Association of Journalists. He lives in Montreal.